Walks of Faith

First publication, November 2019

ISBN: 978-1-7342607-0-0 (Trade Paperback)
ISBN: 978-1-7342607-1-7 (eBook)

Website: www.ElderSteve.blog

Cover Illustrations: Moimoi13 – fiverr

Bible verses are from the NKJV unless otherwise noted.

i

Contents

WALKS OF FAITH
Steven A. Smith

Introduction

A fter walking the faith walk for years and sharing with others some of the journeys the wife and I have traveled, it has been impressed upon me, and encouraged by others to write them down and share them. My wife Belinda, being an equal part of all of this, and my rock I would rely on to keep me focused, kept us grounded in Him, and would not let the world distract us from fulfilling His purpose for our lives.

Now, we were probably the least likely in our families to have such a transformation in God. To abandon all and set out on a series of walks that has spread out to almost a quarter of a century is even more of a testimony. But here we are. God put us together and we have drawn strength from each other, and mostly from Him. The thing about it is we are in no way exceptional people, just your average everyday Christians that God has used in Kingdom work. But God very rarely uses the extraordinary. He gets more praise and credit for using the ordinary. We are living proof that, *"not many wise according to the flesh, not many mighty, not many noble, are called."* 1Cor. 1:26. My prayer is that as you journey through this book with us you'll see God in a new way, and not just see Him in some things, but in ALL things.

Dedication

To my wife Belinda:

Reflecting on the journeys God has taken us through over the past 18+ years now. How ALL things have worked together for the good - how the sacrifices were not burdensome but joyful - how we lived God's principles of sowing and reaping in major ways - the times of abundance - the times of lack, trusting and seeing His provisions - the great, the good, the bad, and the ugly of all the places we've stayed - the leaps of faith - the stumbles - some of the endless days and weeks of ministry work - the exhaustion - the peace we felt and the wars we fought - the tears we shed in sorrow and also in joyous bliss - the times of being appreciated and the times of being used - some of the empty lonely roads we traveled - the times we felt like outsiders, and the times we felt like family - the times our breath was taken away when God moved as only He can - the times we asked "why?" - the times when we "knew like we knew" - the times when we didn't know, yet, just obeyed.

All these times, and so many more has led up to the climactic moments when we have seen souls being saved, and lives transformed by the power of God. That IS the refreshing. That is when we are blessed above all blessings. Those are the worth-it-all moments. That's why we live and move and have our being; to know that somehow we've played a part in someone coming to Jesus the Savior is priceless. To travel this journey with you is one of the greatest and most impactful things that has ever happened in my life, and our steps are ordered by the Lord..... together.

Preface

There are many people I know that have worked at the same place all their lives - lived in the same city all their lives - lived in the same house most of their lives... and there is absolutely nothing wrong with that. Actually, I get a little jealous of them sometimes because moving & starting over is not something I would choose to do or get excited about very easily at all. I would be very content living life like what I just talked about. So, to be upfront, I am not saying in any way to do anything drastic in your life. But there may be some that have felt an urging to move into another chapter of this thing called life by God's leading. God has been knocking at their spiritual door. This is for them especially, but I also believe everyone can be blessed to learn of the ways He moves so miraculously in the lives of His people.

The Apostle Paul wrote in 2Cor. 5:7 *"For we walk by faith, not by sight"*. That is a very difficult thing to do when walking by sight is all we've been used to - when it has been habitual for most of our lives - when the pressures of others tell us to be one way, and the world strongly impresses upon us to be self-sustaining. For me, it wasn't an overnight transition to stop walking by sight. It came in stages, taught and carefully placed by the Master Himself.

Now, it is very hard to describe what it's like to walk by faith. Some will look on you with disbelief or question your rationality. But I have learned to follow my own convictions, and especially the leading of the Spirit of God. Yes, there have been times I've second guessed things, but it's hard to ignore the promptings of the Holy Spirit. It's hard to sit back and act like you went deaf and didn't hear Him speak to you. It's hard to walk out on what looks like sandy ground, wondering if you're going to be swallowed up or stay on top.

I have found that there is no magic formula, or a set of instructions for walking in faith. There is no book titled, "*Walking in Faith for Dummies*". At least, not that I am aware of. You see, every journey is different, unique, and goes at the pace designed for it. Even if there were a book, it could not cover all the possible scenarios, and fully prepare you for what God has planned for you. The Bible tells about many that walked in faith but doesn't really go into detail about what they were fully experiencing or thinking.

As I have shared lots of these stories with others, some people have almost sneered like I was over exaggerating or making these up. Even some of them almost seem surreal to me too as I oftentimes look back on them. But I lived them, and I am still amazed at God's handiwork over it, and the way He skillfully orchestrated it all to synchronize together. God's timing is perfect, and I am almost overwhelmed trying to take all this in as I reflect, and as I try to plan things out to write. Even tonight before I started editing this, I wept because of the Lord's powerful moving in my life.

These chapters are sectioned in times, or seasons of my life. While yes, there are some overlapping and non-mentioned events, if I had to write it all it would take too much of our time. So, I have selected and prayed for God's leading on what to write, and what not to write. I hope you are blessed, encouraged, and get better reception to the Holy Spirit's promptings. Because being in tune to Him is paramount to walking in faith, and then, listening and acting upon His leads takes determined faith. Faith that we don't inherently have right at the start, but faith that is strengthened by exercising it. It's a process. A process we don't take on by our own plans, but by Him directing us every step of the way.

Chapter 1
The Beginning of Journey's

B ack in the late '90s, I was working as a woodshop supervisor in a manufacturing plant making really good money and things were going great. We owned our home and had a houseful with our two cats, three dogs, a ferret, and a mini rabbit. I think we had a hamster or two and a very populated fish tank as well. Also including, and not least in the bit, was our three kids and soon to be first grandchild. They weren't my biological children, but when I met Belinda, I didn't fall in love with just her, but all four of them. I count that as the biggest blessing I have ever received. I am sure most young single men at 24 would never consider an instant family, but it seemed and felt so right, and I accepted the responsibility with loving, open arms. The kids were young when we got married, and during this time they were all in their teens.

When I first got the job at the plant, I was only making minimum wage and at the bottom of bottoms. It was a transitional time as I was starting new employment after being jobless for about six months. I wasn't following God at that time either, and He was probably the last thing on my mind but used that experience to draw me to Him by having nowhere else to look but up. He also used certain people there at the plant. Their witness for Him intrigued me, and secretly caught my attention.

One person was on a job release from prison and was as ornery as can be, but one day he was talking about a church service there at the jail in which he felt the presence of God very strong. I wasn't part of the conversation but was nearby to hear it as he had a voice that carried pretty far. I believe his exact words were that he had "never felt the moving of the Spirit in such a powerful way". That dialog took me by surprise, and I have never forgotten the captivation and the seed planted inside of me that day. That man never seemed very spiritual after that, or even before that, but the impact of him sharing touched me deeply. I had never heard of such a thing as God's Spirit being felt, and especially in a "powerful way". It really got me thinking about God and that maybe there was more to this Christianity thing than I realized.

Around the same time, there was a young man there that used to lead up a Bible study during breaks. I really didn't know him but admired his boldness and the unashamed way he was, as many of us frowned upon them and just shook our heads, mostly because of not understanding I suppose. Now I was brought up in a religious family, but church stuff stayed in the church, and I had never seen it on the outside. Even though I made like they were wasting their time in all this Bible stuff, I still respected their passion and not being afraid of ridicule or being outcasts. It was impactful to see this, and it bore a strong witness within me. Even after 20 years I still remember it well. Not any particular thing in general, but the drive they had to study God's Word outside of a church building and on their own without the formalities. I can still see the group sitting together talking, and the uneasiness I felt when I walked by them which was probably the Father drawing me to Himself as Jesus said in John 6:44, *"No one can come to Me unless the Father who sent Me draws him; and I will raise him up at the last day."*

Then there was another man that came to work in the same area I was in. He was much older than everyone else and had a full head of grey hair yet could outwork most people half his age. His work ethics and hardworking attitude got my attention and I heard through the grapevine that he was a Christian. Every now and then he would come to our group during breaks and one particular time he was sharing how he was blessed buying a house. How the sellers left it full of furniture which they later found out were antiques and probably worth more than the house. He never mentioned the words "lucky" or "fortunate", but instead, I could tell that there was something in him I wanted that had favor behind it. I didn't understand it at that time, but it was God's blessings on him. This too planted a major seed, as I had never really talked to a Christian much up to that time, and it felt kind of weird and awkward, yet it intrigued me at the same time.

Now I had never heard about God purposely blessing someone. We all heard of luck and being lucky. The man could have easily bragged on himself and rubbed it in that he hit the motherload jackpot but seemed to remain very humble about it all. That was another impactful witness to God being active in the lives of us here on this Earth, and that possibly, He didn't just throw us into this world with the mentality that we were supposed to fend for ourselves without any help from Him at all, and we're just here to wing it.

Shortly after, the wife and I gave our hearts to Jesus. I was 30 at the time, and this is the super-short Campbell's condensed soup version. You see my road to Jesus is a very long story, so for now I'm only including the final events that transpired, but we were at a Home Expo show, and a church that was there had a booth. The young man was very friendly, invited us, and gave us some literature. We ended up going to the church because it was nearby and went to the altar when they called for salvation after a few weeks of attending. Belinda was first and then I went to the altar a few services later. My life transformed almost immediately. The first thing that changed, besides the colors in the world which almost seemingly became more intense and brighter, was my speech.

I used to curse like a sailor as they would say. Seemed like every third word was a cuss word, but here I was stumbling in my language now. I felt such conviction that I couldn't cuss even if I tried. The Holy Spirit pierced me every time I was ready to speak profanity. Everyone must have thought I picked up a stutter. I went from sounding like the old cartoon character Yosemite Sam in his "rootin' tootin' sassafrassin's" to Porky Pig's "ebity-ebity-ebity I can't spea, spea, spea - talk". I got saved and it showed! Months later the hair that used to be down to the middle of my back was now collar length. Nobody told me to cut it, I just was impressed by the Lord to do it after reading 1Cor. 11:14. We joined the church, started tithing, and got involved. Now I know tithing is a controversial subject and if you give a tenth of your increase or don't, that's up to you. All I know is it works, and our 90% goes further with His blessing behind it than our 100% without it.

I quickly started to get promotions in the company, knowing now it was God's favor in my life. I went from temporary to full-time - from a woodshop cutter/assembler to a shop lead - being elevated over others that had been there longer than me. But I had discontentment and started searching for other employment. On one such day, I had an interview for a job. I passed the initial application process and had to go in person to finalize everything.

On the way driving to the place, we had our normal 20 minute central Florida afternoon rain downpour/thunderstorm, and while turning right onto a street I got into a car accident.

It was the strangest thing that ever happened to me and I can't explain how it happened. I was on the inside lane of a double right-hand turn lane and wasn't going fast at all. I wasn't gunning the engine or anything like that. In fact, I was probably over-cautious, but somehow I rammed into the van that was on the outside lane. It was like my car slid out of control, like on ice, even though I was barely moving at all. Needless to say, I missed the interview. Nobody got hurt. It was just a fender bender, but it shook me up so much that I felt that it was God telling me or directing me to stay at the job I was at. I ate some humble pie and cast aside the thought about looking for another job, and it probably wasn't two weeks later I got a promotion to supervisor over the entire woodshop. If I had made it to that interview, I would have missed an incredible opportunity and a major increase in pay.

I was so grateful and thankful to God for elevating me because, in the natural, I should have never gotten the chance. There was actually another person in front of me that should have been chosen for the position and was in line for it. They were more qualified, had been there longer, and had favor with the other supervisors in the plant. But in between my job interview car crash and my promotion, the hand of God moved. The person that should have gotten the supervisor's position was transferred to another department, so the option for them had been nullified, so I was their next choice.

God's timing was perfect in the whole situation. His interaction, which may have seemed drastic considering I had to get into a mild car wreck, worked out exactly how He planned it. Some blessings will overtake us no matter how much we try to move in the flesh and choose after our own desires. This was the first time in my Christian walk that I recognized God moving on my behalf considering how strange it seemed to me. His hand allowed me to pursue my discontentment, but also put up a roadblock (crash) for me to stop and consider that maybe I was making a wrong choice. Also, that I should have sought Him in this matter which I didn't. I could have easily called the place to set up another interview and explain my traffic accident, but I had enough of God in me to realize that I wasn't supposed to pursue that other job offer and learned to be content with whatever God had for me.

Belinda was working at Universal Studios at the time and had to take off work for several weeks because of a surgery. She was recovering from a hysterectomy and was starting to do light-duty work. One day she was cutting the grass in the backyard, and there was a small pipe that stuck out of the ground maybe just a couple of inches. I was in the front yard and I heard a loud clunk sound and the lawnmower stopping very abruptly. I ran to the back not knowing what had happened and found her weeping. It took me a while to get any information out of her because of the state she was in, thinking she was upset about breaking the lawnmower, but she told me God was speaking to her as she was mowing and said she was going to "take care of children", and she snapped out of it when she hit the pipe. (By the way, miraculously there was nothing wrong with the mower and the blade wasn't damaged at all).

This was one of her first experiences of such a thing. Yes, God sent nudges occasionally, but she said with an audible voice she heard it, and it shook her to the core. While she was still on release from work we started planning the daycare God spoke to her about, and it seemed obvious that our grandson would be her first child. *Heaven Sent Family Child Care* is the name God gave her, and we had a peace about her not returning back to work at Universal even though this was a huge step of faith. Our finances were unsteady at the time, but peace was all over us, and an assurance was felt knowing that God had this.

So, Belinda started operating what shortly turned into a very successful home Daycare business. We didn't have much startup money, but God was piecing it all together, and she was making key connections. Along with favor with a community coordinated care for children organization, the majority of toys and learning curriculum were donated, and God poured it on the hearts of many to give including our daughter. Soon, a few toys and books in the back room of our house quickly spread to where she had almost too much to keep up with. The backyard turned into a playground that many other daycares would envy. She always prayed that God would give her the children that He wanted there, and He did. She tithed off the business even from the first few dollars in the first week of operation, and I know that's one of the reasons why God blessed it so.

God's favor consumed her to where she even got grants and scholarships for childcare classes. She was able to get a National Accreditation, a Gold Seal of Approval, and drew the attention of many other home daycares that came to her for mentorship. Belinda loved what she was doing and always had Christ as the center of her business and passion. She also had free use of a 15-passenger van to take the kids on field trips whenever she needed if it was available.

As many were the blessings that came our way, we were always and still humbled by God's grace in our lives. Even right now as I am writing this nineteen years later, I am in awe how He moves for us. As simple as catching a ceiling fan on clearance yesterday, and then buying it online to pick it up at a store and finding out it was even $30 less than advertised. Then the next morning finding out we were each eligible for $125 from a credit reporting agency breach settlement. We both stand amazed, and I believe being thankful is key to having a relationship with Him. But not just to receive more blessings. But having a thankful, grateful spirit that shakes our emotions to the core and realizes; He blesses us, He sets things up, and we don't deserve it.

Now Belinda had started to watch and incorporate foster children, as the local department for children reached out to her looking for places to house these kids with nowhere to go. They were at the time inundated with children, and even had kids sleeping in their offices because of nowhere to place them. I remember the day I came home from work and she asked if it was OK to go 24 hours and the next thing I knew they was dropping off children to our house. How could I say it was not OK? We were young, had tremendous faith that God would help us through, and He did. In major ways!

I can still remember the work that went into converting our entire house into a childcare facility. Almost every room was used including our bedroom for the infants. But after a while, I could see the toll it was taking on Belinda. We had help from our daughter and our best friend Mike, but still, I could see her being overwhelmed. We could not say no to taking in kids, but we could only take so many with the house we were at, which was ten foster children.

Then we had six additional regular daycare kids during the week. The house got so cramped over a short time, that we thought best to move into a bigger house and rented ours out.

When I went to work I felt so empty inside and it was like I was missing something, and the huge longing to help my wife was almost more than I could stand. I wanted so badly to leave the job God gave and promoted me at, to help my wife full-time. We looked over the finances and knew it was going to be tight but doable. The more I desired it the more peace I felt about it. I mean in the natural, who would walk away from a manufacturing plant supervisors' position with great benefits and pay. God literally more than doubled my income when I was there, and I gained great experience in leadership and people management. But I was starting to really dread going to work and it was like my heart was breaking every time I left the house. I talked it over with Belinda and she said to do whatever God told me.

Now I warn you ahead of time NOT to follow the path I went down, because your path may be different than mine. God has unique individual plans for all our lives, and we are to find and pursue them. Not imitate what others have done or are doing. We can easily mess everything up God has laid out for us by acting on impulse or being impatient. Or even by delaying and over planning, and not seeking His will.

I got up to go to work, as usual, one day. Dreading leaving the house just to work the grind for some company while there were children at our house that needed love, attention, encouragement, and to feel special as they were adjusting to the major changes they had in their lives. As I walked into work, I felt that my time was expiring and soon I would get the release to put in my notice. I really can't put into words the feelings that you go through when you know God is wanting you to do something; when He has a new plan, and that you will soon get the go-ahead. It's like keeping a secret from everybody and you are getting ready to shout out "surprise!" but have to maintain your composure. Because the last thing you need is for someone to know, and then throw doubt or unbelief your way that could spoil the plan.

So, I got to work and was feeling very disconnected from what was going on there, just lightly taking my responsibilities. All I could think about was those kids and my wife needing help. How I was just wasting away making some company richer while purpose in life was waiting for me at home. All the anticipation and wondering soon turned into a peaceful release. I knew the time had come. I had toiled with those emotions for months and now was the time. I was overcome with peace. The peace that, *"surpasses all understanding"*, that Paul talked about in Phil. 4:7, that guards our *"hearts and minds through Christ Jesus"*.

During my first break, I was at my desk writing a resignation letter explaining why I was leaving, and soon turned it into the vice president. I was going to finish out the day but on my lunch break I told everyone goodbye and that was it. I left right then and there. The plan God had made for me reached completion at that was the end of that journey. I went home with joy in my heart and peace in my spirit. Most people would have been freaking out just contemplating walking away from such a great opportunity and career. Especially not giving any notice, which pretty much severed being re-hired. But I did it. I stepped out in faith trusting that God would see us through and provide.

Now, this wasn't like I was putting Him to the test, but rather, Him putting me to the test. I saw how His hand guided and promoted me at work. How he gave Belinda favor in her business. How she stepped out in faith and followed His leading and He provided. This was NOT a reckless plan I devised, but a road that God set before me that had two options; stay where I was at, or hook into this plan He laid out for us. I believe either option would have had His blessing on it, but option two had the greater blessing attached to it, yet the harder road to follow.

The next little while was some of the most challenging, and most gratifying days of our lives. We quickly outgrew the house and moved into a much bigger one keeping the same amount of kids. God blessed us tremendously in our finances to where we could buy our very own 15 passenger van for the daycare. That gave us the freedom to go wherever we wanted when we wanted. You should have seen us shopping with ten foster kids in Walmart ranging in ages from 6 months to 11 years old pushing three and four baskets. We could probably write a book just on the daycare/fostering experiences and how God helped us to shine His light into their lives. I used to grab my guitar on occasion, and we'd sing some children's Christian songs. We'd also load up the van on Wednesday's and Sunday's to make it to church.

There were many spiritual battles as well, and we'd be in almost constant prayer over the children as some came from very dark and dangerous environments. We'd weep just reading the files on some of them and the trials they had to endure at such early ages which they should have never gone through. But they were happy after some adjustment time, and when structure and loved were incorporated, they flourished.

I used to tinker in the garage making children's furniture and cubbies for the house, and it soon started another business for us. What I learned from my dad and in the woodshop from my past job, soon went from a good idea and turned out as a God idea. *SAS Woodworks* was then birthed. Soon, after some research and development, planning and praying, and a few sales and happy customers wanting more product, it seemed viable to grow more. So, I found a place nearby that was very affordable for the shop and orders started coming in. That pulled me away from the daycare, but Belinda had it under control in the daytime which was much easier in the new house and I was there to help at night.

God performed miracles to get my business up and going as well. The place I found was owned by an older gentleman and I didn't have to sign a lease agreement or pay a lot upfront. I almost didn't get the business license because some of the manufacturing might have been considered industrial, but the person behind the counter took the time to ask questions and deemed just a commercial license was all that was necessary. I was able to get all the equipment necessary through sales and an unsolicited donation (a humbling miracle), and the business started taking off.

I began every day in prayer at the shop, and sometimes I would actually get on my knees. I don't think I ever failed to pray first thing before I got involved with work. As I have reflected back several times, I can see God's hand upon the planning and business side of things. I had everything written down and knew exactly what I needed to make a certain product down to the penny, but this was almost like a God ability to do this. I knew exactly how much material I needed and how to really stretch materials out to eliminate excessive waste. Yes, I learned some things from working at the plant, but this was natural and easy for me. I had even gotten favor with suppliers and costs. It was beginning to be a real company that had potential, and even though I knew I could never keep up with the bigger companies, God blessed the business and I tithed from the profits. In a very short amount of time, it was getting so busy that I could barely keep up. The daycare van also doubled as a shop van, and I would take the seats out and haul supplies or deliver the finished product with it.

We were living what seemed like ideal lives with our businesses and fostering children, and we were also prospering and growing in God. Our living room, with no TV, was mostly for studying the Bible and praying. As Christians for a while, we were so hungry for God's Word and were faithful at church attendance. We listened to Christian radio stations, watched all the powerful preachers when we were able to, and bought a lot of audio sermons and studies. We just couldn't get enough of God and were yearning to know more and more about Him.

Even before the businesses started and before my big promotion at the plant, I would listen to all the popular preachers on the radio at work in my headphones. We were involved in the church, as Belinda would help in the nursery, and I played guitar for the weekly youth night band. When the Bible says in Romans 12:2 *"And do not be conformed to this world, but be transformed by the renewing of your mind, that you may prove what is that good and acceptable and perfect will of God"*, that was us. We were not the same. Not even close. We were transformed by the renewing of our minds which radiated God outwardly from us. I am not saying at all that we were the poster children for new Christian converts, but I don't think anybody that knew us could dispute the changes, as we changed with Godly changes. To Him be the glory!

During this season we faced many obstacles too. We learned how to really trust and depend on God knowing that as quickly as it all came, it could quickly go too. I think many get too comfortable in the blessings and forget the source of it all and the One that holds it all together. The main thing I remember from this time is I never felt that this was it. That we arrived at our destination and that we were at our prime.

Even from the time the first foster child arrived, and the first SAS Woodworks item sold, I felt that all of it was temporary. Now don't get me wrong, just because deep inside of my spirit I felt this, it didn't diminish my passion and desire to put 1000% effort into it all. Words can't really describe, and I don't think I can ever express how it feels to be living the dream knowing that one day it could all change by God's hand. It's like being torn in two directions: one is settled and content and the other is anxious yet apprehensive about what lies ahead. In the midst of it all was the peace that only comes from having a personal relationship with Jesus. I can say even from then until now, which is over 20 years, the *"peace that surpasses all understanding"* (ref. Phil. 4:7) is a tangible real experience that nothing on this Earth can compare to.

Chapter 2
Sell Out!

T here is always a pivotal point in life that gets you to pause, decide, and move. In my very short-lived basketball career in grade school, we learned how to pivot, or what is called the pivot move. This is where you plant one foot firmly down and your whole body rotates around that foot in the direction desired. There has to be mighty strength and certainty in the pivot move to gain an edge on your opponent for it to work effectively.

We would practice this move frequently, and the way we did it is we'd pick which foot to be the pivot, and then we'd take the other leg and swing our body to the position we wanted to go to. At no time the pivot foot was to leave the ground while spinning on it because it would slow the move down and a foul could be called for traveling. Worst yet, the opponent would get the ball from you. You have probably seen a player holding the ball, pivoting back and forth trying to pass-off or look for an opportunity to take off running. Sometimes it carries on for a while until things fall into their place, or it is a quick, precise, and deliberately planned move with perfect results.

Pivotal points in our lives are either initiated by us or by life's circumstances coming our way. We pause, look at our options, decide what move to make, and then go with it. Joseph, the beloved by Jacob his father in the book of Genesis, had many of these experiences and most of them were from bad circumstances hitting him straight on. He chose the course of action he needed to take which was always a humble attitude and faith in God. His pivot move could have been of bitterness towards Him, or revenge for his brothers and many others that sold him out, but instead, he kept his foot firmly planted on God's promises and dreams for his life and rotated his focus towards his Lord.

I think about Matthew the tax collector in Matthew 9:9, and Jesus walking by his office and simply saying, *"follow Me"*. The Bible records it, yet it is not mentioned in any other Gospel except his. Matthew had a pivotal point to consider when the ball was thrown to him. He didn't go into details but imagine the talk afterward when he got up and left his career behind. He had to have seen the Master before, and possibly longed to follow Him, but didn't know how it could ever happen. Then Jesus only spoke two words and he arose.

His co-workers must have thought he lost his mind. Maybe his family did too but his mind was made up. He could have just sat there and acted like he didn't hear Jesus - or said maybe he'll follow after he gets off of work - or maybe just a simple, "I can't because I have too much to give up" - and this excuse and that - and "I'm not worthy" - and "what will people think of me?" - and "I should give a notice of some kind"…… We have no idea what was going through Matthews mind, but I do know exactly what was going through his spirit and heart. Peace! Not peace that the world gives, but the peace that only comes from the peace giver, Jesus. (Ref. John 14:27).

I know because the wife and I lived it for ourselves and not just once either. It's the kind of peace that shuns everything the world is screaming. The peace that knows! The peace that knows, like it knows, like it KNOWS! That peace is the ground under our pivot foot - our rock that we stand on - our strong tower - solid ground and not sinking sand. Without our foot firmly planted on it, we can't change directions or even fake the enemy out and make our move, but instead, we could stumble.

Many have slipped and fallen flat on their face because of uncertainty. Because of following the popular masses instead of hearing the voice of God and using His peace as a guide. Even though they had a good idea, and all seemed right, there was uneasiness and no peace. That's the difference between a good idea and a God idea. God ideas have assurance and peace even though they may contradict everything surrounding it. I believe Matthew spoke volumes by just getting up and following. He didn't just blindly make a rash decision, He walked into certainty, with certainty.

Belinda was taking care of the kids as usual one day, and it was lunch time at *Heaven Sent Family Child Care* on this one pivotal afternoon. Normally in our house, the TV is very seldom on, especially when feeding the kids, and we didn't even have cable just the ole rabbit ears antenna. But she felt a strong compulsion to turn it on this day, and as she fumbled through the few channels we had, she heard a voice that pierced in the airwaves and caused a sweet hush in the house. It was the voice of an anointed Prophetess of God from Canada with words of encouragement, and she spoke into the lives of callers phoning in for prayer.

My wife told me all about it when I got home and I can remember the excitement in her voice as she kept saying, "we've got to go, we've got to go!" Of course, I was confused and was prying out as much as I could, but it was slow coming, but I finally understood what she was talking about and how she badly wanted to go to this revival in town to see the Prophetess from Canada.

Now we weren't quite babes-in-Christ Christians, but the whole Prophetess/revival thing was totally new to us and even though my initial thoughts were of caution, I somehow was drawn to all this. I didn't hear or see what Belinda did on TV, yet her excitement got my attention. And even though I couldn't go that night, she asked if she could get our good friend Mike to go with her. I had no objections and I think in the back of my mind, or maybe I spoke it out loud I don't remember, I felt she should be careful to attend and put a guard up because we know sometimes the devil comes dressed in sheep's clothing. But she came home even more excited than when she left and told me all about it, and then I was really interested. I really don't know anyone that has a sharper sense of discernment than her, and if she felt OK about it all, that was good enough for me.

So, the next night I went and for the first time in my life I witnessed and felt what my co-worker at the plant called, "the moving of the Spirit in such a powerful way". From the air being charged and thick with praise and worship, with people raising their hands - some in joyful tears - some trembling with the power of God on them - words of prophecy were spoken over many including myself...

Now I was raised Catholic, and we got saved in a Baptist church, but this Pentecostal thing was vastly different, yet felt so natural to us. First I knew about Jesus, then I knew Him personally, now I was feeling the Spirit He promised to us in the book of John 14:15-18 when Jesus said in regards to the Spirit of truth, *"but you know Him, for He dwells with you and will be in you"*.

For so long I always thought about the Holy Spirit being *"with"* us, but never realized that He could be *"in"* us. It almost seems kind of mystical and yet humbling that God would put His Spirit in us. They didn't teach me that in my Catholic upbringing, but it was implied that God was up there in heaven, and access to Him was pretty much non-existent. Neither did they mention in the Baptist church that God was *"in"* us, but only *"with"* us. I didn't put all of this together back then and not until sometime later, but I felt God and felt His presence very strongly.

This just wasn't an isolated one-time thing either, but that revival lasted eight or nine weeks and I only missed two of the services. So that translated to well over 40 services I attended in which I felt the presence and power of God in all of them. Those weeks could probably be a book by itself, as about halfway into the revival the prophetess' dad joined her, but my emphasis in all this isn't the revival itself, but how God orchestrated things and timed them perfectly to get us to and through the next faith walk.

During this time, the department started to find homes to place children into, and some even got to return back to family. It was bittersweet, and there were a few we even considered adopting ourselves, but they weren't available to be adopted because their parent(s) still had rights. Within a few weeks, all of the foster children had left, and our assignment had ended to care for them. I know we call them foster children, but in the department's eyes, they were just long-term daycare children. What was strange is they never approached us to actually foster these kids, but just looked at it as them being in a daycare full time. It was definitely an unusual arrangement we had with them, as we were foster parents on paper, but we weren't. To those kids though, we were Mr. Steve and Ms. Belinda, and we gave them every ounce of love we could give and taught them the things of God.

So, Belinda was back doing regular daycare Monday thru Friday with just a few children. It was an adjustment for all of us as the big house we were renting became empty of kids at nighttime. It got lonely, but we were getting more and more involved with this revival and started helping out in the services. As we look back we can see how God was strategically putting everything together. We grew exponentially in the things of God, and if you have never been in a Pentecostal revival, things are led by the Spirit and not by a program. They just don't teach how to flow in the Spirit in Sunday school or in a sermon, it's learned by tapping into the power of the Spirit while the Spirit is moving.

There was a connection bonding between us and the ministry team from Canada, like when you haven't seen someone for years and then you meet back up and take up where you left off. It was kind of like we didn't know each other in the flesh, but in the spirit, it seemed we were long lost friends. We just knew we were to be together with them. As the revival continued there was mention that they needed a professional video camera, and

God provided the exact one they needed by someone donating it. A brand new one. With my background in audio and video, they asked if I would run the camera, and there was no thinking about it, I gladly did it and was excited to do it.

Among the many miracles we had seen during this time, two stick out the most because they were with loved ones I knew personally. Belinda being the first, and she had always had back issues for as long as I knew her. During one of the services she was called out for prayer and the prophetess' dad said that he saw what he could best describe as Holy Ghost insulation wrapping around her spine. Much like you see insulation on water pipes. He had no prior knowledge of her having two disks out of place, but God revealed it to him.

He then sat her in a chair and held her feet straight out, and one leg was noticeably shorter than the other. He prayed a powerful prayer and commanded through the power of Jesus that she be made whole. The shorter leg instantly extended out, and both were the same length now. I am not sure what happened after that, but she came under the power of God and was slain in the Spirit and fell out for quite some time. Now I know Belinda, and for her to fall out like that was not something pretended, but I know God overshadowed her and His presence and power caused her to fall to the ground.

I have experienced falling under the power many times myself, and as much as people want to say it's fake, I can attest, it is real. Even in the Book of 1 Kings 8:10-11 it talks of the priests that could not minister because the glory of the Lord filled the house of God. Even when the soldiers in John 18 were asking

Jesus if He was the Jesus of Nazareth they were looking for, His words, *"I am He."* caused them to fall to the ground. The presence of God is real, and to experience it in a powerful way is not only breathtaking, but it resonates a joy deep within that for many including myself, brings uncontrollable tears.

Belinda got back up off the floor and said she felt much better, and it was explained to everyone there that sometimes healings are a process. For some, yes instantly, other times, no. So, the service continued, and we went home, and in the wee hours of the night she woke me up, which usually isn't an easy thing to do, but she asked, "do you feel that?". I felt such a presence of God in the room and it was like we were just floating. Then she asked, "do you see that?". I opened my eyes and the room was completely illuminated, but there were no lights on. She weepingly said, "it's the glory of the Lord and He's touching me". I fell back to sleep somehow, and in the morning she said the glory was there for hours and she knew her back was completely healed. I went to give her a hug and noticed she was a little taller. I looked down but she didn't have shoes on. God realigned her spine and healed those vertebrae so that she grew an inch.

The other miracle I referred to was with our first grandson. He was around four and was due to get his tonsils taken out. We occasionally took him to the services, and he had fallen asleep for a while, and then woke up and walked up to the front for prayer. It seemed kind of unusual, but the prophet asked what he would like prayer for. We told him and thought he was going to pray for the surgery, but he said God was showing him something to do with his brain and that God was going to heal it. He then prayed powerfully over him.

A few months prior to that, our grandson was out playing in the driveway when I heard what sounded like a hammer hitting concrete. I looked and he was getting up off the ground and instantly on his forehead it looked like a golf ball emerged. He was checked out at the hospital, but they said he was OK and sent him home. The bump slowly returned back to normal so there was no outward sign of the trauma. Now, there is no way the prophet could have known of his head injury, but Belinda and I both strongly believe, God healed something unseen from the doctors. She mentioned he was a little bit slower after the fall but was back to his normal self after prayer. God knows and God shows.

Now it's really hard to explain, but we were feeling a connection with the ministry that would go beyond this revival like our relationship wasn't going to end. So, before we knew it the revival had come to completion, and what a time in God it was. Our lives were forever changed, and I know we jumped a few levels in faith. As a confirmation to the connection, we were invited to join them in another city about three hours away for a few services, and then in another city about an hour away after that meeting ended.

I can't remember exactly how it transpired - maybe we were in our living room - maybe in the kitchen - but Belinda came to me and very confidently said that God told her we were to "sell out". I looked at her as anybody would I guess, like she was crazy! I was puzzled and almost in disbelief. But she was very adamant about it and acted like I was supposed to jump on board right then and there. "Sell out?" I asked her. "What do you mean?". "I am supposed to close down the daycare and you are supposed to close your business" she announced. I almost wanted to rebuke her but saw in her eyes and heard in her voice that she fully meant what she said, so I just pondered on it for a while. I mean, serving in the revival was powerful and purposeful, and that was definitely life-changing; but to sell out, and I wasn't quite sure even why yet?

The next day I was hoping she'd forgotten about it and wouldn't bring it back up, but before we even got started with our day she insisted that she heard God tell her that we were to "sell out!" I really didn't know what to think, but I know God spoke to her before in the backyard while cutting grass, and heard Him say that she was going to "take care of children" - and how God made miraculous provisions for her to do that for a long time - and how He blessed us with that business. I felt some peace in it, but the flesh took over and I think I grew numb for a day or two trying to process it all.

We just kept this to ourselves and never discussed it with anybody. She approached me again about it and said she was going to close the daycare. My mind was spinning like she had lost her mind, but my spirit was attentive and receptive. Peace was starting to consume me, and I finally said to her that she needs to obey God and follow her convictions, and we both instantly felt the peace that surpasses all understanding. So, she started giving notices to the parents and a few weeks later it was completely closed. Her pivotal move just happened, and her foot was firmly planted on God's peace.

As far as my situation, God was dealing with me, and witnessing Belinda's obedience was beyond inspiring. I prayed at work, and prayed some more, and stayed almost in continual prayer over it all because I wanted to hear it from God for myself. I went from totally shunning the idea - to considering it - to feeling a tug - to fighting inside and battling the pros and cons - to laying it all down to God and crying at the altar saying, "Lord, thy will be done".

I was starting to feel that I should close the business, but you know how it is to second guess things and want super solid confirmation. Almost like wanting angels to appear out of heaven, sounding their trumpets, a heavenly choir singing, and the voice of God thundering over all the Earth the answer. But we all know God doesn't move like that much. If He did it would be too easy. We wouldn't have to really, deeply, seek Him. Just phone a friend and get their opinion or go get a word from the nearest prophet. That would be ideal, right? But Godly wisdom and directions are not instantaneously deposited at our commanded wishes, it's given when we seek it, and the seeking is not a one-time event, but a continual inquiring.

We have to *"ask"* Him for the answer. *"If any of you lacks wisdom, let him ask of God, who gives to all liberally and without reproach, and it will be given to him."* James 1:5. He gives it freely and doesn't look down on us in shame shaking His head, making us feel inferior to Him. He is there waiting for us to *"ask"*, and that word ask doesn't mean to demand; but to crave, desire, and require. In other words, we don't need the Godly wisdom as an additive to our decision making, but as a requirement and an integral part of the process.

Also, it says in James, *"But the wisdom that is from above is first pure, then peaceable, gentle, willing to yield, full of mercy and good fruits, without partiality and without hypocrisy"*. James 3:17. Now, do you see any double-mindedness in that verse? Exactly! That wisdom doesn't come to confuse us and get our thinking in an uproar. Now, really break it down and read that verse slowly and repeat reading it until you fully get it.

When we make decisions on our own and leave God out of it there is almost always confusion, uneasiness, anxiety, and turmoil in our thoughts. Is that any way to make a life-changing decision feeling like that? Of course not, but sometimes we do that because it's easier to make a rash move than seek God on it and wait patiently for Him to speak, because we think what we want is want He wants.

So, one morning after getting up from my knees praying at work before I started my day, I felt in my spirit that I was working on my last order. The same feeling I felt when I walked into the plant at my other job and God's peace surrounded me. Leading up to this it seemed the phone calls stopped. No inquiries at all. No new orders lined up. I remember just staring off at nothing and thinking about the way things transpired, and that the time had come to close *SAS Woodworks*. There was that peace *"which surpasses all understanding"* again, that guarded my heart and mind through Christ Jesus. (Ref. Phil. 4:7). I wasn't sure what the future held for my career, but I knew that God had a plan, and for us to find it, we had to end this one. The leading of the Spirit is not a leap into the unknown, but a journey to the unrevealed.

I came home from work that day and I remember looking at Belinda and smiling, and she gave me that look like she was thinking, "you finally got it!". Yes, I had got it. The answer I didn't know needed an answer to, because I never would have gotten to this point without a spark of God's supernatural wisdom. So, I told her that God said for me to close my business. This was about a week to two weeks after she closed hers.

Everything seemed to be moving so fast but at a pace that we could keep up with. Nothing was hectic about it at all. Nothing took us by surprise or blind-sighted us, we just followed what we were feeling in the Spirit. This revival was life–changing... no... spirit changing for us. We were being schooled and learned so much, so fast, about God and His ways. This faith walk was in motion and we had no idea how God was going to move next, but only that He was moving.

The Spirit was telling us that we were going on the road to travel with this ministry but there was very little indication that God was speaking to them, except for a few invitations to meet them at nearby revivals. Yes, we knew we were helps, as we were already making flyers for them, helping with newsletters, and I was videotaping the services when we were together. But we felt so strongly about this as we just closed both our businesses down and was starting to sell, giveaway, and bless people with everything we owned including business items.

As I look back on it even right now I think how we KNEW God spoke to us. I mean to forsake all and move by faith and not by sight involves huge faith, not just a hunch, and we were just waiting for God to continue to reveal His plan(s) for us. So here we were engulfed with God's peace and moving towards something that didn't seem tangible in the natural, and the miracles God was performing was simply amazing. We were Matthew's rising from the tax table following Jesus because He simply said, *"follow me"*, not because we were coerced into it by man. Not because it was all planned out in advance. Not because we had a huge bankroll we could skim off of when the finances got tight. We were literally walking by faith and not by sight. (Ref. 2 Cor. 5:7). We grabbed hold of God's hand and let Him lead the way with our spiritual blindfolds on.

The house we were renting was empty now and we needed to get out of the lease somehow, because we could no longer afford the payment. We couldn't move back to the house we owned because another family was staying there. So, the landlord came over and we were explaining to her that we needed to move and get out of the lease, and we could tell she wasn't happy at all. We were current in payments but the next month was fast on top of us and we didn't have a clue if we were going to be locked into paying off the lease, or what she was going to do about it, because we needed to move out.

So, we were finishing up the conversation, and she was getting ready to leave when I heard the Spirit say to ask her if she would take the refrigerator in lieu of a payment. This fridge was only a few months old and top of the line. We had also bought a new dishwasher. I was fighting with asking, as I thought it would make her even angrier, but I couldn't ignore the promptings. So, with a certain fear of rejection, I asked anyway. I offered to let her keep the fridge and dishwasher in lieu of the following month's rent and to my shocking surprise, she agreed. Praise the Lord! We had another month to spare. Rent was paid!

Now the next dilemma was where were we going to move to? We were both unemployed, and how were we to get another lease? The Lord spoke to me again and said that I was to ask our landlord if she had any other properties nearby that had cheap rent. Boy, I fought with that prompting and wrestled with Him on it, thinking to myself that I was going to get the chewing out of a lifetime. So, I called her after the Lord wore me down. This time though I didn't have as much doubt, and actually was excited to hear possibly a positive answer even though I knew it could go very wrong. She answered, and I ask if she had a more affordable house nearby with reasonable rent. She paused for what seemed like a very long minute and said that she did and gave me the address. So, we met up with her at the place.

They were in the middle of preparing it, and it needed painting inside, and the backyard was a jungle. So, the Lord gave me another idea. "What if we move in the way it is now, complete the painting, and clear out the backyard for you?" is what came out of my mouth before even thinking about it or asking Belinda. She smiled and the deal was done. Even she felt it was the Lord's doing and the other place immediately rented out, and we downscaled into the new place. God worked a miracle in that situation. We got out of an expensive lease - found another place - got a more affordable payment - and even kept our same landlord. Everything was falling into place as we had most of our belongings gone by now except for the essentials.

So, there we were. We followed the Lord's leading but there was still a huge part missing in all of it. We went through all that effort just on direction and peace from the Lord. We could have ignored the calling - let flesh decide our future - tucked our tail between our legs and ran from the promptings - but we un-regrettably decided to sell out, and we did all of this before we had confirmation or even an invitation to help the ministry full-time.

We were busy painting, cleaning, and clearing yard debris; and I was to say at the least, getting very anxious as we were waiting for God's next move. It seemed almost agonizing to wait and then it happened. Now Belinda had to remind me of where, but I already knew how it happened. We met with the ministry for a meal at a Steak N Shake diner, and I believe the exact words they spoke were, "we want you both to pray about joining us on the road full-time". Belinda looked at me and we both tried to hold back our smiles and told them, "we don't have to pray, God already spoke to us a few weeks ago".

So, it was official. The Lord confirmed what all of us were feeling. It was a time of great rejoicing and we were in awe that God would choose us to help work alongside powerful people of God for the winning of souls and to see revival go forth. We shared with them all about how God prepared us for it, the many ways He moved, and the faith walk we had just walked. We were all astonished at the Lord's moving and how everything came together. They even shared with us how they were kind of apprehensive about asking us but felt strongly it was the Lord. Yes! It was definitely the Lord behind it all.

Chapter 3
On The Road - The Beginnings

T he excitement was stirring along with a sense of great humbleness, that of all the people in this world, God would call and choose us. I mean, who were we? We had only been saved for a few years now and I am sure there were ones more qualified God could have spoken to. Even in the revival, there were many that loved God as much as us, if not more. But why us? We felt so underqualified and hoped we could live up to the ministry's expectations, and especially God's. Maybe He had called others? Maybe they didn't answer? Other Matthew's - *"Follow me"* - but maybe they looked the other way and felt they had too much to give up? Why was it so easy for us, even though we wrestled in our minds some? Well, lots. We didn't want to be away from our family. We loved what we were doing in life, and God blessed what our hands touched very much, but I guess the key is knowing that He is responsible for us. If He asks us to do something, the responsibility is on Him then, and not on us.

Matthew arose from the tax table and walked away from it all, Jesus then became responsible for him. When Jesus says, *"follow me"*, it means we are not responsible any longer for ourselves. Now don't get me wrong, we still must do our part, but if He wants us to drop everything (sell out), He will then provide everything for the journey. When we start that faith walk as directed by Him and walk away from it all, He is obligated to care for us, and plans on taking care of us. He doesn't say to follow Him and then realize He didn't think it through enough and made a mistake. He has a provisioning plan already in place. Now that should boost some faith right there.

So, before we could leave to go on the road, we had to get quite a few things in order. We still had two of our three children living with us and the youngest was getting ready to turn 18 in a few months. We had no intention of just abandoning them and leaving them to fend for themselves. That was not an option, but we did have to pray a lot about this. The pull of God on us to travel on the road was definitely a Matthew calling, but we knew that we would be home occasionally. That kind of eased the worrying, but as parents we always feel guilty when we are not around for our children. We want to be there for everything.

Now, the house we just moved into was fully furnished. New paint on the walls. A well-manicured backyard. The bills were all paid, and both our sons knew they had to do their part to help with the bills. After all, they were living there and it seemed they had no problems with it, as the bills and rent were affordable, and we promised to send money to help. They were probably excited to have the house to themselves and be on their own without parents around nagging them. Everything was good to go except for the car that we had. Someone we knew said they wanted it, so we let them have it and they took over the payments. It was all falling into place and we knew it was the Lord's doing.

The 15 passenger van we had, which served well with our businesses, was getting ready for its third purpose. Ministry. I took out the last seat in the back, and that section of the van now turned into a cargo area for the computers, video camera, personal belongings, and clothes. All that we owned now was in that van, as everything else was no longer ours. We divided up all the furniture and household items to our three children. Yes, all. We downsized to the point where most people probably would never dream of doing. I had even sold my custom-made electric guitar and custom-made bass, along with my guitar amp to a music store. I did it gladly, as we needed the money to put all of this together to be able to go on the road and have our kids provided for.

Nobody from the ministry asked us to do any of this or influenced us in any way. This was our Godly conviction, our own doing, and our calling we knew we had to answer. And yes, there were many sacrifices we made and did, yet none of them really hurt. Not even selling my music equipment. I think my wife cried about that and was saddened over it a lot more than me, but it just felt right to do it. A few years later we really related to the verses, *"So Jesus answered and said, 'Assuredly, I say to you, there is no one who has left house or brothers or sisters or father or mother or wife or children or lands, for My sake and the gospel's, who shall not receive a hundredfold now in this time-houses and brothers and sisters and mothers and children and lands, with persecutions-and in the age to come, eternal life"*. Mark 10:29-30.

So, there we were. Serving in the Kingdom. We had already been in dozens of services where people were healed, delivered, and set free from strongholds in their lives. Many were elevated in their faith, experiencing as we did the power and presence of God. But the greatest miracle of all was, and still is, salvation. That's what I looked forward to and enjoyed the most in a church service, somebody accepting Jesus as their savior. Or maybe someone coming back to the Lord after straying away and renewing their faith in Him. Those were and still are the worth-it-all moments.

We were doing it. Actually, traveling and staying in cities for the sole purpose of evangelizing and bringing revival. We didn't have a home to go back to every night, we stayed in hotels. Literally living out of suitcases. It was more than "walking in faith" as we had to pray in everything and depended on offerings to meet the needs, we were "living by faith".

It's one thing to "walk" in faith when there are other avenues around that we can always fall back on, but "living" by faith is dependent upon God providing all our needs at the time the need arises. We lived every day with the work of the Lord in front and everything else last. We didn't wait to get everything in order and inline, we just followed the Spirit's leading and fully trusted that the needs would be met. We didn't have a huge budget we could dig into or was sponsored by anybody. God said go, so we went, and He met the needs along the way.

There were some times that the offerings were very good, and other times where it cost us money, leaving us with barely enough to make it to the next city. Lots of sacrifices. Lots of struggles. But one big God. The wife and I were paid a very small salary, and most of the time in the first years, there was hardly anything left to pay us. But we were OK with that as we told them from the beginning to always meet the ministry needs first, and then if the finances were there, then they could pay us. There was a time when what they owed us was a substantial amount, and we felt led by the Lord to sow that back into the ministry and cancel their debt to us. So, we told them what we wanted to do, and I know God blessed our personal finances with that offering and even to this day, I believe we are still prospering from that seed.

So, our first traveling experience took us to southern Georgia into Cordele. This was also the first revival that Belinda & I headed up all the upfront work between the newspaper, radio ads, and radio programs. As well, we worked with the host Pastor organizing everything and in this revival, because his church was quite small, we rented out a meeting room. We spent a few weeks there and then I believe the next city was Adel, Georgia. During the services, I would run the video camera, and then we would make the services available on cassettes and VHS video.

This was before CD's and DVD's became the mainstream media choice. We only had one VHS recorder, so I had to use the camera to play the tape to record onto VHS. This was our humble duplicating department along with a home dubbing cassette deck. Belinda would help with the printing and cover designs for the tapes, as everything was done from her computer and printer. It was all in-house, or should I say in-hotel. It was budgeted tightly, and we used minimal resources for production.

If we weren't busy in the services, which was usually six days a week, we were making tapes and I was editing together radio programs with excerpts from the services. I had a very simple editing program for audio, but we had nothing for video. Back then there was no such thing as an affordable video editing program for a PC computer. Plus, our computers were not anywhere close to the top-of-the-line to support such a thing, but it's all we had, and we made the best of it. We managed and it worked, but it consumed a lot of our time.

The ministry leaders said that we could have the tapes sales profits, and it helped to supplement our wage and send money back home. We were earning our way, so to speak, and it felt great to be a blessing in the ministry and to the Kingdom of God. We didn't sell a lot, but it definitely helped. Eventually, over a few years, the media department started to support itself and we could buy supplies and equipment through profits too.

The next revival was in Ft. Lauderdale, Florida, and this one meeting, which lasted months, was probably one of the most memorable. We had so many blessings come our way personally that brought tears to our eyes because we knew God was behind it. Usually, in these types of situations, the evangelists gets all the attention and the helpers just seem to blend in with everyone else. But God had people single us out to be a blessing to us. From Pentecostal handshakes (if you ever had one you know what I'm talking about. It's when someone walks up to you to shake your hand and in the process indiscreetly slides money into your palm and says, "the Lord wanted me to bless you"). People were even tipping us at the tape table.

Now when we left to go on the road we didn't have a big wardrobe or church clothes so to speak, but people started bringing us nice clothes. New clothes. Dresses for Belinda. Suits for me. And some even took us shopping for clothes. It was such a humbling experience, and one time I remember Belinda telling someone they didn't have to, and they said, "yes I do so I can get my blessing. Because God told me to do this". God was moving on our behalf and spoke to many people to bless us, and this was just confirmation that we were in God's will for our lives.

After that, we had a very short break and went back home for the Christmas season, and then our first road trip to Canada was on the calendar. After we left Florida we stopped by my parents in Kentucky first and stayed with them for about a week. Trying to explain to my Mom and Dad and assuring them that we weren't in some strange cult was very challenging. They were strict Catholics but were actually open and supported us even though they may not have agreed with our new Pentecostal beliefs.

I remember my Mom asking, "do you really know what you are getting into?" They were dumbfounded at the fact that we closed both our businesses to pursue this. We had no formal training or went to a school of evangelism, nor had we graduated a Bible college. All we had was God directing and speaking into our spirits to go. Before we left there to drive to Toronto, we had someone notice the front tires on the van were kind of thin and offered to pay to replace them and do a front end alignment. We were humbled again. We knew God was behind it and we shed many tears of joy.

I know it was way out of church protocol for this age, or not even halfway rational in the sight of the world's view, but God said, "sell out" and we went. Some might have thought it reckless on our part, but for us, it was nothing less than following God's unction in us and walking in faith like we were born to do this. It felt so natural. We lived our lives for 30 years with no faith in God and lived like we wanted too. Then within a four year period, we were sold out - blood bought - Bible reading - church serving - tithers - altar workers - evangelistic helpers - full-time media team travelers - spreading the Gospel and bringing revival in the US and Canada. "Had to be God!" is what some church mothers would say. "Had to be God" is right, because never would we have ever dreamed or conceived that we would have been doing that.

Our first journey outside the USA was just about ten hours away. God had led us thus far and we knew His hand would continue to be upon us. We were the furthest away from home we had ever been and still had lots to go. I must say the first time crossing the border was nerve-racking as we really didn't know what to expect. Lots of questions to answer and telling them we were on our way to help a ministry in Toronto raised the man's eyebrow pretty high, but he let us through with no issues.

Everything seemed so different. km/h instead of MPH on the road signs. I had to quickly learn to look at the small numbers on the speedometer. Gas seemed really cheap until we saw it was sold in liters and not gallons. The money was not what we were used to, and no paper one dollar bills. They had one dollar and two dollar coins instead. A Loonie and a Toonie. It was nice to pull out a pocket full of coins and have lots of money.

Toronto was a shocker and the biggest city we'd ever been in. I quickly learned to drive aggressively because courteous drivers were not there. Waiting for someone to let you out into traffic didn't happen. So, finding a gap and lunging out was the only way I learned to get into traffic. Most people didn't have a problem slowing down for a big white, full size extended van pulling out in front of them.

We adapted well and settled in there and spent several weeks in revival in the Toronto area, and the next place was in Quebec. That was like a country all to itself. Everything is in French and most everyone spoke French. Nothing like a Kentuckian ordering food in a drive through. It was almost comical trying to get people to understand with my accent. In the services, we had a translator and that was quite an experience too. I now know how it feels to be the minority and not be able to speak the common language.

What struck me the most is that no matter where you are at - what language is being spoken - it is the same God and the same Holy Ghost power being manifested. I must say as much as I love God's people, and souls giving their heart to Jesus and being transformed, I was glad when we were getting close to leaving there because it was very hard not knowing any French and living there, even temporarily.

It was close to going to the next revival and the van was starting to have some issues with going into reverse, and then it started taking a long time to go into drive. We were praying that it was just low fluid but it wasn't. The transmission was starting to give out and here we were in Quebec, and if we weren't with the hosting Pastor who was bilingual, we struggled to communicate. But someone at one of the services found out that we were having van problems and said they knew somebody connected with the church we were at that had a transmission shop.

We didn't have that kind of money for a transmission repair but then someone else stepped up and said they would cover the bill. After the initial inspection, the repair company called and said it needed to be rebuilt or replaced. We were kind of stuck there in Quebec now with our van needing major work done and a revival we needed to get to. The same person that said they felt led to pay, said they were going to pay the entire repair bill no matter how much work it needed. They just wanted to be a blessing to the ministry and insisted to do it, and didn't want us to pay them back. God had provided again in a huge way.

We found out that it was going to take a few weeks for the van to be ready, so we had to rent a van. I don't remember how it happened, but we got favor with the rental place and they said we could rent a van for the time needed, and they were going to waive the mileage. This was a big deal because our next meeting was in New Brunswick which was about 600 miles or 900 km one way. God's blessings were overtaking us.

I can't count how many miracles we had seen, or how many people came to the altar for salvation, but it was a lot. Nearly every service. I remember when we first started I would keep a mental count in my head for the number of people that accepted Christ in the revivals starting from the revival we first attended which was over 350 souls, and then it quickly got up to 500. After that I lost count.

Being on the road and living by faith was extremely hard, but the worth-it-all moments of seeing people weeping at the altar, giving their lives to Jesus gave us joy that revived strength in us. Ezra, in the book of Nehemiah chapter 8, read to the people the Law of Moses and they wept at the hearing of it. Probably because they felt they didn't measure up to God's standard. None of us do. I'm not sure how many times I wept in a hotel room because I felt I didn't measure up to the task of serving great prophets. It was exhausting, and with all the responsibilities Belinda and I carried, from - being driver's - communicating with host pastors - making housing arrangements - meeting room arrangements - advertising - graphic design - tape duplication - audio editing - preparing radio programs - serving in the services six days a week... it was overwhelming at times, to say the least. But when the altar calls came and souls were added to the Kingdom, strength came, and all the burdens became much lighter. His joy, the joy of the Lord, strengthened and renewed us.

So, we were in Canada for a few months, left New Brunswick and picked up our van in Quebec, stopped in Kentucky to visit my parents for a short visit, and then headed back home to Florida. Now during our mission work in Canada, everything changed in our home front. Our house that we owned and were renting was behind in payments because the tenants got behind and moved out, and we had no way of getting caught up.

The house was going into foreclosure and Belinda came across a company that buys houses for cash. We were traveling full time now and it didn't make any sense to try to keep the house even if we could. So, after owning it for 11 years, we made the call, and they gave us an offer to pay it off for what we owed and with very little profit on our end. We probably could have fought with the pricing now that I look back on it, but we felt it was God's hand on this and followed His lead. This was also a way to protect our credit as well, so we accepted the offer. The closing was set up and I remember staying in the house until then, which wasn't long.

The night before I don't think I slept at all. It was uncomfortable anyways because we slept on a pile of blankets on the floor, but this night I remember just laying on my back reflecting on the many years we spent raising our kids and grandkids - the mornings we would wake up and everyone would pile into our bed and just talk and laugh including most of the pets we had - the renovations we did - the satisfaction of being a homeowner - the place where our lives were transformed through Jesus - how Belinda built the daycare business there…

It was bittersweet. Lots of tears were shed that night and deep down in our core we knew this was the way to go. Us quitting the ministry to get full-time jobs to save our house wasn't an option. Paul wrote in Philippians 3:13-14, *"Brethren, I do not count myself to have apprehended; but one thing I do, forgetting those things which are behind and reaching forward to those things which are ahead, I press toward the goal for the prize of the upward call of God in Christ Jesus"*. God had great things ahead of us and we knew we hadn't arrived yet, but that we still had much further to go in Him. For us to reach for the things ahead, we had to get free from *"things"*, as there was/is an upward call we were following.

We did it. We sold our house and I remember pulling away from the Title company and quickly parking and both of us weeping. That house meant a lot to us, and so many great memories resided there, but it was just a house and it is long gone now, but the memories still remain. As I look back on it all I wouldn't change a thing. Selling out meant exactly what God said. Everything. So many don't ever completely fall into God's calling because they are still holding onto something He said to let go of. It may not be something as big as a house - it could be a habit - a friend - a job - traditions - invented beliefs… God is pulling them to Himself and their purpose, but they won't let go of *"things"*.

There is a prize as Paul said. Not sure what it is but I don't want to miss out on it? Maybe it's just self-fulfillment in knowing we are running the race and pursuing the upward call. Paul also said, *"I press toward the goal"*. Sitting in an easy chair waiting for God to put wheels on it and drive us to our calling isn't going to happen. *"Press"* means it's going to hurt sometimes. There are going to be sacrifices. We will have to let *"things"* go.

If that wasn't enough, the hardest thing about being on the road for us, especially Belinda was being away from the kids and grandkids. We wanted to be there for them, help them, support them, and now that we were Christians we wanted to be a living example for Him in their presence. She was weeping as she had done often, missing them and wanting to be there for them in their trials. But this time she was almost inconsolable. She told me that God had spoken to her that we were to turn the kids over to Him. To fully entrust them into His care. She used the words that she was to "lay them on the altar". Not in a sense of abandoning them and not helping them in the physical, but to stop worrying about their needs. That was His responsibility now.

God confirmed to us later through a prophet, that because we sowed our lives for the winning of souls into the Kingdom, He was taking care of our family - that as we were taking care of souls by serving Him, He was taking care of our kids - that as we were ministering to other families, He was taking care of our family. It was reassuring and humbling to know that God was giving our kids some extra attention as we served full time in ministry away from them.

The big 15 passenger full-size van was getting a lot of miles and wear and tear after traveling in it for some time, and for the driver and front passenger, it was to say, the least comfortable vehicle you can imagine. So, while we were home in Florida one time we decided to go looking for a newer vehicle. The problem we had was in financing. We made a very small salary, but our housing now was provided by the ministry, and since we used our own vehicle they helped to pay for it and the insurance. The problem was trying to explain that to a car lot and getting an approval for a loan. They would hear our story and almost get mad for wasting their time. But we had faith that God was going to give us favor and step in for us.

It doesn't matter what it looks like on the outside when faith is rising on the inside. David didn't look at Goliath, he looked at his own God. That's how he won, and we made up our mind too that we were going to win. We knew God was going to work on our behalf and a refusal from a car lot just meant that's not where God's favor was. It was out there somewhere. We just needed to find the right dealer, on the right day, with the right salesman, with the right appraiser for our trade, with the right finance person, for the right vehicle... Sounded impossible, but with God all things are possible.

So we went to the first dealership and we had a certain style vehicle in mind (and it wasn't a full-size van you can bet) and we test drove a few, but nothing really caught our attention and they pretty much dismissed us after we told them our employment arrangements with the ministry. The next dealer had something we sort of liked and dismissed us too. Something about saying you work in the full-time ministry loses people from wanting to help you. This didn't discourage us, but more like just frustrated things.

We knew God would intervene and give us favor, but He was working on our patience as well. Over the course of a few weeks or so we visited a total of eight dealerships only to go through a long process of finding a vehicle, test driving it, appraisal for our van, explaining our pay and allowances we had in the ministry, paperwork... only to get either "no" or "you're going to need a lot of money to put down".

Then one morning we woke up and felt to go visit another place but in a different city south of us. Something about this time felt different. Remember in Matthew chapter 9 when the two blind men were following Jesus and He asked them *"do you believe that I am able to do this?"* What was their response? Was it "maybe", or "not really but we hope so"? No, it was, *"Yes, Lord!"* And then how did Jesus respond at first? Did He heal them just because He had the power, and simply because He could? Of course He could, but He asked if they believed. So then why did Jesus delay, and why the question? I believe He wanted to test their faith level first. Jesus wanted to hear a definite, affirmative *"Yes, Lord!"*.

Now even though Jesus didn't ask us directly if we believed He was able to give us favor at a car lot, our faith level and action to go and try for the ninth time answered, *"Yes, Lord!"*. I mean most would have given up after trying just one or two times. I know it seems very irrational, but every time we stepped foot on a car lot we weren't "trying" to buy a vehicle, we believed it was already done.

The two blind men must have believed their blessing was already done, otherwise they wouldn't have caused such a scene to *"cry out"* (scream or call aloud is what it means in the original language) while following Jesus to His next destination. They didn't stand on the side of the road in one place but traveled and followed Him. An effort went going forth. Then, they imposed on Him at the house He was staying at. That's determination! Every time they cried out for Him to have mercy it counted as an attempt. Jesus didn't need to ask them what they wanted; He already knew. He could have very easily talked to them on the road but waited until He felt the timing was right. I believe He was certainly testing their faith, but also their patience and persistence as well. Jesus told the blind men, *"according to your faith let it be to you"*.

So, Belinda & I prayed like we always did that God would give us favor and the right salesman. We did the usual browsing, but we were up front with the salesman and told him our income situation and I really can't remember if we had any down payment. He didn't seem to be phased and we test drove a few vehicles, but nothing excited us. I was getting kind of frustrated as the vehicle we finally chose, something wasn't right in the paperwork process, and came back that it was a no go. I looked at Belinda and she could see I was not happy at all because I felt like they were playing us. Something in our Spirit didn't feel right, but then the salesman had a look like he had another idea. It was like a light bulb turning on and he said that he had another vehicle that was on special. It had "get it out the door pricing" on it.

So, we followed him through the showroom and walked out the doors to an outside showing area. There was a brand new 2001 (this was in the year 2000 now) fully loaded GMC Jimmy Diamond Edition. He said to us, "I believe I can get you into this one with your trade and the rebates on this". So, we took it for a test ride and guess what? We ended up driving it home. God had come through spectacularly and left us in a state of awe. He had moved on our behalf and gave us a much, much nicer vehicle than we were expecting. The old van served its purposes and was such a blessing, but the Jimmy was so much more comfortable.

God simply amazed us in the ministry beginnings. We were both proud and humbled of how God moved for us. There really aren't any words to describe knowing that God personally intervened on your behalf. Some can dismiss it as luck, or claim the efforts for themselves, but faith walks have an assurance attached, and brings a grateful confidence in the One who guides their steps.

Chapter 4
On The Road - The Long Haul

I t seemed that we were living in an almost surreal world as things were moving so fast, and we could barely keep up with the blessings, miracles, and doors God opened up along the way. I am sure there are many I have forgotten, but we never forgot to give Jesus praise and thanks for each and every one of them. Even to the smallest of things. We loved what we were doing and humbled by it all that God would work all things out for us to serve in a ministry that loved souls as much as we did. We had heard it preached many times that favor with God exceeds far beyond man's ways, but to now live in His favor was almost mind-blowing.

Another one of my favorite verses is, *"Now to Him who is able to do exceedingly abundantly above all that we ask or think, according to the power that works in us"*. Ephesians 3:20. Now, He is *"able to do"*! When it looks like all is hopeless - that there are no more avenues to trod - everybody has given up on any chances for things to work out - He is able! Not only able, but He will do *"exceedingly abundantly above all we can ask or think"*. He won't work with our fickle ideas but will create new ones and shows us ways we'd never thought of. Complex plans that are executed perfectly.

That sounds great and wonderful, but many, including myself, have neglected to really grasp the last part of that verse *"according to the power that works in us"*. But wait, I thought it was God's power? It is His power, but it's in our power to release Him to work in our lives and situations. Now, God has enough decency to be on standby, but will not position Himself into our situations unless we give Him the power, or authority, to do so. That's the mistake some of us has made, we want Jesus to help but only give Him so much, or should I say so little to work with. We want Him to do it our way, or the way we think He should do it, but for Him to do exceedingly abundant things, we can't put limitations on Him and only give Him a little to work with. We have the power to give Him full reign, and also have the power to give Him nothing. It's according to the power that works in us. Our faith.

So, we were getting ready to go back on the road again, but felt we needed an apartment. The house we arranged for our sons to live in was no longer an option, as they both moved out with different friends. The extended stay hotels were affordable back then, but we needed a home base for when we would come home. Once again we faced the challenges of explaining our income, and this time to a realty company that manages apartments. We had a specific area in mind that was convenient and affordable. So, we applied and just believed that God was going to do it again like He did with our new truck.

The more we were seeing God move for us, the more our faith was elevated to believe he would work things out. There is a certain confidence level that arises when you know God is working on your behalf. In the flesh, we knew we probably didn't meet the qualifications to get an apartment. But in our spirits, we knew and felt He was going to do it, and He did. Our little one bedroom tiny apartment was our new home base. Our youngest son moved in because his new place fell through, so it was perfect timing, plus we weren't really going to be there much.

Our next road trip I believe was in Alexandria, LA and we stayed a few weeks there before going to Texas. We spent a lot of time in the Lone Star state, as it seemed the ministry was needed in a lot of cities there. Pastors would be talking to other pastors, then those pastors would reach out to us to come to their churches. One of our favorite cities was Odessa. There was a church there that sat probably 250, but their Sunday services would only have about a dozen or so people. The minister's got on the radio and we also bought some TV commercials, and before long the place was almost full every night.

Revival broke out and the miracles were numerous. Many gave their lives to Jesus night after night for weeks and weeks. There was a really nice hotel there and we got great rates and loved it. We had stayed in some of the worse hotels you can imagine on the road, and for us to stay there felt like we were royalty or something. Our room was like an apartment.

By this time, we had upgraded our video and cassette tape duplicating gear. Somebody had given us a high-speed cassette machine and we were starting to increase our VHS tape recorders to where we had three or four. I would videotape the services and we'd get back to the hotel and make tapes. The one thing we were really lacking was a newer computer for the video editing program. The one we had was very slow. A half-hour TV program would literally take eight hours or so to process, and I usually set it up to do it while we slept.

It was mentioned at the church we were at, that we were believing God for a new computer. There was a dear couple that we got to know pretty well, and they told us they wanted to buy us a new one and felt led by God to do so. We were praising the Lord and most of us had tears in our eyes when they came to tell us. God was doing it again!

I had to drive about an hour away to Lubbock to get the computer because no stores in Odessa or Midland carried it. I can remember the ride there and back, and the overwhelming love I was feeling from God. Just writing and remembering it is tearing me up right now. Not only was it one of the fastest computers out, but it saved me so much time and I could do better quality work too. That eight hours of processing now only took about an hour and a half. I had put a sticker on the computer monitor with the couple's name who bought it for us, and every time I would see it, I would say a prayer for them and thank God all over again.

Then it hit me, and in that hotel room I wept and wept as God reminded me of a certain day when I was working back in that plant before I became a supervisor. I was pretty new to the faith, yet this was another moment I'll never forget. I was cutting wood as I normally did and listened to all the morning preachers on my radio headset. This one particular morning though I was thinking about my Pastor, and what it must have been like for him to do Kingdom work and not have a regular job. What it must have felt like to be in full-time ministry. I contemplated this for a while, and it was almost like God was planting a seed in me because I remember it so vividly. I believe God was preparing me then even though that thought was just a faint desire.

I really can't put it into words, but the thought of serving full time sparked something deep in my spirit. It was seared into my memory. So, in that hotel room, as I stayed up late video editing, I realized I was now living that impression God put in me. I was now serving in the full-time ministry and there is no way I could have ever planned it - applied for the job - or studied for it. God directed my every footstep to this very point in my life. To say I was overwhelmed would be an understatement. The seed He planted in me was in full bloom.

In Proverbs 3:5-6, it says *"Trust in the LORD with all your heart, and lean not on your own understanding; In all your ways acknowledge Him, And He shall direct your paths"*. Yes, He shall and will direct your path, and that's what He did for us. It's amazing how we can go back through His word and find something that had already came to pass over our lives. We may have read a passage several times before, but then revelation jumps off the page and a witness comes into our spirit.

Now we didn't read that verse and apply it as a formula to get into full time ministry, we just lived what this is saying with no intentions of any gains, but simply because we loved Jesus and God's word. Solomon wrote it as an admonition and as a warning, because if we read the opposite of it and add in "do's and don'ts", and take out the "not's", it would read: Don't trust in the Lord with all your heart, and do lean on your own understanding; In all your ways don't acknowledge Him, and He shall not direct your path. I know we don't deliberately add the "don'ts", but when our faith is minimal or we are double-minded, we do, and He can't direct our paths.

It's also extremely hard to trust in the Lord with *"all"* our heart. Flesh still has some doubts present, and we still want to hang onto what we know and what we are familiar with. It's natural to feel this way at first, but the more we acknowledge Him in everything and let go, and let Him take over, we find ourselves leaning more to His knowledge which is far superior than ours. He then directs our paths.

Have you ever driven through a highway construction zone late at night, and all the cones and barricades are directing which path to drive down? Almost like driving blindly. I've done it before and was kind of scared as it looked confusing, but I still stayed on the path they laid out trusting I would get through it all safely. God has it all laid out for us too, but we have to trust Him - lean on His infinite knowledge and wisdom - and acknowledge Him in everything we do to find the paths He wants us to take.

God knew that one day my experience in the audio/video field would be used for His work. I had absolutely no idea, but that's why He gave us so much favor in getting me into Full Sail University and planting us where He did after I graduated. Even before I was saved, He was working in my life and was waiting for me to one day come to Proverbs 3:5-6.

Now, to backtrack a little bit and expound on some things since I brought it up; before I was working in the plant, I was a professional recording engineer for around six years. That's what originally brought us to Florida but one day it all came to an end. I got laid off because business was slowing, and it crushed me. That was, at that time, the best job I ever had and in one minute it all ended. I could have gotten employment in the same field, but I would have had to move which wasn't an option because the kids were still very young and settled, and I didn't want to uproot everything.

Then what seemed like out of the blue, I got an offer at another studio in town because I knew the owner. He even gave me the keys and alarm code to go in and familiarize myself with the equipment before I took a session by myself. Then one Sunday morning I went there by myself, and as I was in the big studio room where the musicians set up, I felt a heavy presence come upon me and I started uncontrollably weeping and feeling that I wasn't supposed to be there.

It literally brought me to my knees, and I cried uncontrollably for about 45 minutes. It was like oppression was pushing me down physically, and I knew after I got up that I definitely wasn't supposed to pursue this venture. I was left with a "what now?" wound in my life. It was traumatic for me and I was shaken from it for a long time. I wasn't saved at the time, but I felt it was God behind it all in some mysterious way. That's when I hit rock bottom and after being unemployed for a while, I got the job in the plant as a temporary worker.

I thought all my audio engineering background was in the history books, and it was, until God called us to the ministry about four years later. That's why I wept so much in that hotel room. Because I realized that He had something better and more rewarding waiting for me in the audio/video field. Being laid off from the recording studio crushed me almost beyond repair. But God sees the end from the beginning. Something inside of me died back then, but He resurrected it back to life for His purpose.

Your dreams may have been shattered and buried, but what if God has a resurrection plan for it for His Kingdom? Or what if what you were pursuing was way off course from what He has purposed for you? Either way, there is so much joy in being on the path He has directed for us.

Texas was hot. Some days the outside temperature on the truck gauge read 107 degrees. So, it was a bittersweet day when we started heading north towards Canada. We were going to miss it there but wasn't going to miss the heat. So, part of the ministry team was staying there in Texas while we joined the Bishop, the prophetess' dad, and drove north to their hometown and church in Regina, SK. Canada. We had heard them talk often about all the great people there, and now we were going to meet them in person soon. Now, I don't remember the exact chain of events in Canada, but I will never forget some key times.

Lodging for Belinda and I was always an adventure so to say. Sometimes we would be in a hotel, other times in people's houses, but this time they found us a trailer home in an RV park which was on the outskirts of town. Whatever was in the budget we were thankful for, and were blessed to be able to come along and be a part of this move of God no matter where we stayed. This trailer had a living room, kitchen, a bathroom, and a bedroom. It was like a home away from home and we loved it.

I bet we weren't there for maybe a day or two and we were preparing for a weekend camp meeting on an Indian Reservation nearby. The meeting was in the town community hall and I was responsible for all the audio there. I just jumped right in, my nerves were going crazy as it had been a long, long time since the last time I ran audio, especially in a live situation. But all the training and experience I had just naturally came right back, and I managed everything almost effortlessly it seemed.

There were many Gospel bands playing, and it felt so natural for me as I faced many audio problems but very quickly solved them. All the worldly experience I had was now being utilized for Kingdom work. The dream that died was reborn and I wept again as God's plan for my life was unfolding, and this time under the anointing and in His presence. That weekend was exhausting between the driving back and forth, hauling equipment, and setting up and tearing down. Belinda was such a huge help as I was on audio and she was videotaping. We were/are a team of our own and always have been. We were made to serve together.

We also rented recording equipment for the music, so I really was on double duty between the live sound and multitrack recorder. The goal was to produce CD's of all the music, and while the hard part was done with the services and recording, there was still a final step. I had to take several hours of music and mix it down to CD's and we were on a time crunch. We had to get the equipment back to the rental place the next day. So, after the Sunday night service we loaded up and headed back to the trailer. I unloaded all the recording equipment and set it up in the living area. I don't think I even had a chance to eat that night as I was excited yet stressed to get all the postproduction done. I spent several hours getting the sounds and blend of instruments just right, and as I just sat back and listened, I began to weep. Yes, I never wept so much in my life until I got saved, as knowing Him is such an awesome experience with Him being interactive in our lives. Tears of joy like I never had before.

So, as I listened to the music I flashed back again, like in the hotel room in Texas, knowing that all my recording experiences led up to this moment in my life. When I thought my dream job was buried years ago, God restored it - when I once wept in anguish of losing a once in a lifetime job, God gave me tears of joy of restoration as my talents were now being used for the Kingdom. I think I even woke Belinda up and shared my revelation with her.

Pressed for a deadline to meet, I stayed up all night and kept at it until late morning. The joy of the Lord was my strength along with the anointed music from the camp meeting. I am amazed how God took a sinner like me - closed a career door - took me through some things so I could get saved and get to know Him - and reopened it for a more rewarding door.

After that camp meeting it was back to our newly found normal in Canada. It was a typical Sunday service at the home church in Regina, but the outcome was far beyond typical. The anointing was so strong in the place and the Bishop was helping to sing with the praise and worship team. He started singing *The King Is Coming*, but after the first verse he was overcome with grief and cried. Then he sang it again a second time. The verse goes:

"The marketplace is empty
No more traffic in the streets
All the builders' tools are silent
No more time to harvest wheat
Busy housewives cease their labors

In the courtroom no debate
Work on earth is all suspended
As the King comes thro' the gate"

I can't remember everything he spoke as he was prophesying, but the main thing I remember is he was looking into the heavens as in a trance and said, "I see four, what looks like anti-aircraft missiles, just firing, and firing, and firing, and firing into the air". It was powerful, and I really can't tell you anything else that happened in that service. He prophesied a lot, but this time was memorable, and it etched into my spirit.

A few days later Belinda and I were in the trailer, she was in the bedroom and I was in the living room. She felt she needed to turn on the TV and she did. I heard the loudest gasp I ever heard come from that room, and she said with a troubled voice something to the effect that the US was under attack. My very being was pierced, and as I got up and started walking down the hallway I heard in my spirit, "it's just the beginning". When I finally reached the bedroom, which almost seemed like everything was in slow motion, I saw the horrific scenes on the TV. The World Trade towers were spewing up smoke like chimneys and we heard the phrase "terrorist attack on US soil".

Belinda uttered "this is what the Bishop saw on Sunday" so we called him, and he confirmed that's what God showed him but dimly, and not in any detail. The four missiles he saw firing and firing were the four hijacked airplanes used as weapons by the terrorists. Now it made perfect sense why he was singing *The King is Coming* and couldn't get past the first verse. The World Trade Center is the marketplace of the world - traffic stopped in

New York City - everybody that was near a radio or a TV ceased working and was fixated on the news of the attacks - people were waiting for rescue updates - all government offices were closed - all US airports were shut down and planes were grounded for days - all US borders were closed. Panic and vulnerability were controlling the minds of probably everybody, wondering if this was it, or was there more to come.

We couldn't go back to Florida even if we wanted to, but we got ahold of our family, and there was a peace inside of us that God was watching over them. They were all OK and would be OK. The Holy Ghost spoke to us that we were to stay right there in Canada and that all would be well. The ministry asked us several times if we wanted to go back to the States when we could, but we knew we didn't have to. That God was watching over our family.

You see, God put it into our spirits when we first started traveling that as we were taking care of other's families for the Kingdom, He would take care of our family. And He certainly did! Now don't get me wrong, it wasn't like we didn't want to run back to them as soon as possible, it was more like a feeling that God would have them better than we could ever try to. So, we just continued in Canada and left our family in His care. Some may not understand or agree with our decision, but faith walks are not always conventional or meet the popular consensus.

While the trailer was nice because we didn't have to stay with anyone and was like a home to us, winter was starting to kick in and we knew we wouldn't be there much longer. The RV parks close because of the extreme cold as there is no way for water to run in/out of a camper. It was already starting to get colder, and because we were from Florida, we had very little winter clothing. Belinda had brought our winter leather coats we never worn much before, but that was all we had. No boots. No scarves.

While we did have a bathroom in the trailer, we had to take showers in the community bathroom area. It wasn't heated and the hot water didn't stay hot for very long. It was starting to get really cold and Belinda had no gloves still, as we had no money at that time. Living by faith is just that. Living by faith. We literally prayed in almost everything we needed, and Belinda needed some gloves. We shared mine, but it broke my heart that I couldn't provide her with something so simple.

Now this is her testimony and I hope she doesn't get mad at me for telling it, but it was another cold morning and she walked down to the showers. Her hands were freezing, and she was praying that God would make a way for some gloves. Now around this time we were the only residence on site besides the owners, as everyone else left for the Winter, so we had the place to ourselves. Belinda was coming back from her shower and as she entered the trailer she was weeping, but yet had a smile on her face at the same time. She held up her hands and there were gloves on them, and she wept even more while putting her now glove covered hands on her cheeks to wipe away the tears.

She said that when she walked down there everything was as white as can be with the fresh snow on the ground. She got into the shower and when she got out there were the gloves just lying there on the windowsill by her stall - nobody around - nobody else there - not even any other footprints in the snow on her way back. She said, and I believe her for this to be true, that "God had an angel leave them there for me". We both rejoiced at His provision and that might have started what Belinda refers to now as "a hug from God". Over the years since we have gotten uncountable hugs from God. Not all material things either. It's unfortunate that many go through life and never recognize them and dismiss them as luck or coincidence, except for maybe the big ones. I know I was guilty, but was now seeing Him in all things.

Over the next few months we traveled back to Toronto and spent more time there in revivals, but mainly to video tape several courses the Bishop was teaching at the Bible college. The drive there was actually quite relaxing as we weren't in a big rush and stopped in a few places along the way. The views in a lot of areas were majestic especially around Lake Superior. I took many pictures, and we stopped at a rest area that overlooked a waterfall which a walking bridge crossed over it. I don't remember exactly where it was, but the landscape was beautiful and memorable. There were many times traveling in Canada where God's creations and landscapes just took our breath away. We cherished those times seeing all of that, and then throw in some bison or moose, and maybe a light covering of snow.... Heaven on Earth for sure.

Now in Toronto, the Bishop taught in the daytime and then we attended services at night. The wealth of wisdom we received from those classes were priceless. We learned so much in a very short amount of time and received certificates. We never really had much "formal" Bible training or ministerial training, but the "hands-on" training we accumulated can't be taught in a classroom. To be able to flow in the Spirit in the services came from experiencing firsthand, but also because the Bishop would take the time to explain and train us informally.

Just casual conversations, asking questions while driving, or having lunch would turn into a mini-class so to say. Some preachers/evangelists are unapproachable and almost shun you for asking questions, but the Bishop encouraged it. He believed in discipling, and it showed from the many ministries birthed from under his leadership. He rightfully had earned the name "Bishop" as a title, but it was also the name we always called him by which he respectfully earned. So many have a title now days but no fruit to back it up. But Bishop was a Bishop and more. He was our spiritual father and took the responsibility of training us up in the way that we should go in ministry. He unselfishly poured into others for the furtherance of the Kingdom. He used to say, "it doesn't matter who has the microphone as long as the job gets done".

While staying in Toronto, someone let us use their vacant house they had. It was such a blessing to be able to have a kitchen too. I know that may sound strange, but when you are constantly on the road, you eat out a lot and it gets old pretty quickly. But for us to have even a tiny fridge or a microwave while we were traveling was extremely welcomed and a luxury. I remember times when even a bowl of cereal from our hotel room was much appreciated over a sit down meal or a drive thru. We were definitely spoiled in this big house with a full size kitchen for sure. We could go out and eat if we wanted to, not because we had to. I will always cherish the time there, the many saints of God we met, and the Biblical education we received.

Belinda and I drove back to Regina by ourselves and Winter was in high gear. This time driving around Lake Superior was different, as the Lake was frozen in some areas and people were out on the ice. I'm not sure I could ever do that but there is beauty even in Winter when the trees are barren from leaves - When the lakes and ponds are frozen over - When the evergreens are white with snow - When the air is refreshing to breathe in.

Nightfall was beginning and we were getting tired from traveling all day and were starting to look for a hotel to stay in for the night, but it seemed they were all full or not worth stopping to look at. So, we made up our minds we would keep driving but the roads were hilly, and snow was falling. The roads weren't treacherous, but we were driving with extreme caution. Getting stuck behind a semi-truck was probably a blessing as we just followed the taillights because visibility was getting worse. But eventually we lagged behind because we didn't feel comfortable going as fast as they were. The lines in the road were getting harder to see and I was not liking these hills any longer, but we knew it wouldn't be long before we got back on flat roads.

As we were coming to the top of the next hill, which was a really long right turn, something caught my eye and I had to brake hard and cut the wheel some and behold! There was a bull moose standing in the middle of the road, and as I crept past it, I noticed his head was taller than our truck. He didn't seem phased about it and we were happy it didn't end with us getting into an accident.

There is a saying we learned in moose country that goes something like this, "hit a deer with a car. Kill the deer. Hit a moose. Kill the car". I can see why too. A deer weighs maybe a couple hundred pounds and a moose can weigh over a thousand. We always prayed, and still do for God to give us traveling mercies, and He definitely answered that night. As tall as that moose was he would have very easily gone through our windshield. God held back the lions for Daniel in the den, I know God made that moose stop in his tracks and gave us favor that night.

If the timing of us meeting him was even a few seconds off, or if he didn't stop when he did, or if I didn't see him and react like I did… well, I'd rather not think about it. God was behind our safety and I praise him for it. I remember it shook me up so bad that we never made it to the flatter roads, but the first hotel we saw we stopped and stayed for the night. It wasn't the nicest roadside hotel, but it had a vacant room and we thanked God for it and for favor on the road.

We made it back to Regina after the long trip from Toronto and got favor at a brand new hotel on the outskirts of town. They gave the ministry a great monthly rate but after a few months the manager wouldn't let us keep that rate and raised it. I believe after that we stayed in someone's house for a few weeks until the ministry got a studio apartment for us near the southside of town. Seemed like we were almost always living out of suitcases and moving all the time but for once, we felt like we had a home even though it was tiny.

There wasn't much in it at first. We had an air mattress for a bed and that was our furniture. A precious church member, who was also one of our spiritual mothers, bought us some kitchen items and her daughter bought us a brand new little dinette set. She was so good to us and fixed us homemade meals often. I had found a perfectly good dresser someone was throwing out by the dumpster. We had everything we needed and were blessed. We stayed at that apartment all through the winter up into the next fall and during that time we stayed busy, busy, busy.

Camp meetings on Indian Reservations were many, and we traveled way up into Alberta and many other Reservations in Manitoba too. The heart of Bishop's ministry was for the Natives there in Canada and we experienced firsthand the hopelessness they lived in. Alcoholics as young as 11 years old, and teen suicide was common among them as they felt they had nothing to live for. Bringing the Gospel to them was so joyous as many of all ages would give their lives to Jesus. We even got to meet ministers and Pastors that were saved under the ministry we served, and heard many testimonies of the power of God transforming their lives. Next to that was the awesome beauty of the Northern Lights dancing across the skies proclaiming God in all His Glory that He is God! There is nothing like it.

The ministry was also on a Canadian TV station now and had their own TV program that aired on Sunday's, not just locally but Nationwide. Belinda and I would also man the prayer lines during the broadcast as we got calls from all over Canada from people wanting prayer. God was using us in so many areas of ministry. It was probably the best times in our lives, but it didn't come without many sacrifices though.

Having our housing paid for by the ministry, and also our food was definitely a tremendous blessing, but then the small salary we took never really went far. Most of the time that got sent back to our family to help them out. But God amazed me how strangers would give us Pentecostal handshakes, or someone would fix us a home cooked meal. Numerous hugs from God wowed us constantly. Who would have thought that selling out would lead these Floridians way up into Canada into sub minus temperatures? I thought -25 degrees was cold until I felt -40 one day.

These two people, (Belinda & myself), that wasn't raised in the church - didn't have any family members in the church - lived however we wanted to live for 30+ years - were probably the least likely among our family and friends to have such a transformation and abandon all to serve in the full time ministry. There were many though in the Bible that were the least likely too, but God chose and used them. Saul, the persecutor of the early church is probably the best example of a sinner that had a head-to-head encounter with Jesus: He then led that same church he once tried to annihilate to a firm foundation and wrote two thirds of the New Testament encouraging and empowering them. We should never underestimate the least likely even among our circle of people.

One Sunday afternoon on an Indian Reservation near Wabasca, Manitoba under a tent (this was in the Summer now) we were going to support a young preacher on our ministry team. Now in some services there would be a testimony time where people that were called on would share an encouraging word, or maybe a praise report about something the Lord has done for them recently. Well, my fear was realized, and we were called up. I was never comfortable speaking in front of people up to that time. In fact, it would almost terrify me.

So, as I started getting up out of the chair, I noticed I was reaching for my Bible which I never did. I couldn't explain it, but I grabbed it anyways and went to the front. My wife shared an encouraging word first, and when it was my turn, I also started sharing. The previous couple of days I was reading a few verses that I couldn't get past. I would try to read on, but I couldn't. So, the next thing I knew, about ten minutes or so had went by and I was sharing was God was speaking to me.

This was totally unrehearsed, but I had just preached a mini-sermon, but before I could sit down I heard in my spirit two words, "altar call". I fought with it for a second or so, but I couldn't ignore it as I heard it again and with a greater urgency. So, I obeyed God even though I could have been rebuked by the hosting pastor there, because this was unprompted and not on the program for the day. But it was prompted by the Holy Spirit. So, five people, mostly young, came up front and gave their lives to Jesus. I had just experienced being led by the Spirit of God for His glory. The service then went on and that young minister preached powerfully, and more people came to the altar that day.

Now keep in mind, I was not a minister. I was a media, behind the scenes guy. No prior training and I was always scared to take the mic. I was available and He used me. I was in tune with Him because I was in His word and in prayer daily. Maybe you have had an experience where you felt something not of yourself leading you. That's the Holy Spirit. Our Helper that lives in us and guides us. We were never meant to walk this walk alone – by ourselves – in our own strength – so that people can give us praise. These feelings, or promptings, need to be acted upon. Not resisted and pushed aside.

We may never preach in a service, but we may share some one-on-one with a troubled soul that needs Jesus. We may not know the words, but the Holy Spirit does. Let's not forget that we are empowered by Him to do His will for our lives. This verse is not a suggestion, it's a promise! *"I can do all things [which He has called me to do] through Him who strengthens and empowers me [to fulfill His purpose—I am self-sufficient in Christ's sufficiency; I am ready for anything and equal to anything through Him who infuses me with inner strength and confident peace.]* Phil 4:13 AMP

It didn't take long for Bishop to hear about my preach/testimony, or what I like to call a preach-imony. We were all praising God that souls were saved through it, and I was tearfully humbled over it and glad it happened the way it did. You know how it is when people have to talk you into doing something out of your comfort zone? And they almost have to throw you into it? I believe because of my fear of speaking in public that God had to throw me into it that day, because I probably wouldn't have done it on my own or even by people begging me to. God threw me into the waters that afternoon and made sure I didn't drown. He gave me everything I needed and empowered me with boldness and confidence. Even after 16 years I still know that it is He that anoints me and gives me confidence to take the mic, and then fills my mouth with His encouraging words.

We went back to Regina for a long stretch as the cold months were coming upon us, and the very first week there I was asked to preach the Sunday morning service. That afternoon in the tent started my preaching ministry and Bishop and everyone in the home church encouraged me on. To think I'd ever be in the full-time ministry was one thing, but to preach and minister at the pulpit was the very furthest thing from my mind. I guess some people know from their youth they are going to be ministers, while others like me, God has to prepare us in His own way and just throw us into it. I think that eliminates any chances of telling Him "no" or backing out and making excuses. That Sunday morning, I surprised myself probably more than anybody else. God showed me, without a shadow of any doubts, that I can definitely do *"all things"* through Christ.

Over the next several months we were heavily involved in the home church as we stayed off the road. Now I have always had a musical background, so I was glad when they asked me to play drums, even though guitar is my main instrument of choice. God was just amazing me, that all the worldly talents I had was now being used in worship. I played drums for many months and also played in a few revivals at the church as well until the drummer came back from being on the road, so I switched to acoustic guitar for a while until the keyboard player went on the road for a bit.

So, the worship leader there heard my banging on the keyboard one time and encouraged me to start playing in the services. Now I knew very little how to play but knew the notes and a few chords so he would help me along with the chord progressions. Before long I was banging out chords with my right hand and bass lines with my left. I wasn't the most skillful at playing that's for sure, but I was quickly learning and getting comfortable playing keys.

During a few prayer meetings I would get on the keyboards and play softly in the background, and every now and then I would find myself singing. To be straightforward, singing is not a strong talent at all, as I only have like a one octave vocal range so there are very few songs I can sing. In fact, I never sang in my life until I was there in Canada, but I was kind of enjoying it especially when I figured out what songs and keys I could sing comfortably in. So, during the services I played keyboards now and the song leader taught me how to flow in the Spirit in the music ministry. He never had a song list so to say, he just played what he felt the Spirit was leading him to minister in. It was incredible to not have a programmed song service, and the services flowed heavily in the anointing and ushered in the presence of God.

Then it happened. This was another life changing ministerial moment for me. About five minutes before a Sunday night service one of the church ministers came up to me and said the worship leader wasn't going to be able to make it, so I was going to have to lead the worship. I was almost in a panic as I quickly thought about what songs to do and the next thing I knew I was doing it. I was leading praise and worship. God had prepared me for this moment and just threw me in again just like He threw me into preaching, and I don't mean that in a bad or disrespectful way. I couldn't say no even if I wanted to, but God anointed me for the moment and the service went very well.

I was amazed how God used me that night as I never would have thought I'd be leading a song service, and really never thought I'd be singing either. You see, God had a different plan, and without Him orchestrating it the way He did, I think I would had been extremely hesitant to even try preaching or worship leading. I believe there is something in each of us God wants to use for the Kingdom. It may not be in the pulpit preaching - it could be in a prayer closet interceding - church nursery - volunteering for outreaches - ushering...

As I said previously, we literally had to pray in everything, even in the home church when we weren't on the road. The ministry did provide our living expenses, but most of the time it was a struggle for us and them financially. Sometimes God would wait until the last second, but He always provided and came through. We were living by faith, and to be living in a different country, and our only source of income came from the ministry, made it hard sometimes as we went without occasionally. I'm not talking about the necessities, but there were very few times in a long stretch of time there that we had any extra money. I am not complaining at all, as we were blessed beyond all we could ask or think just seeing lives transformed by the power of God.

Sister Gerry, a dear lady that had compassion for the hungry like none other we have ever met, ran a soup kitchen in the downtown area and would attend church services when she could. Now, we didn't share with anybody our needs unless someone asked us directly, and around this time we were believing God to provide for us because we were making things stretch as best we could. So, after a service she said we could come down to the mission the next day and get some food, but we would have to help serve the lunch time crowd there. So, the next day we showed up and helped in the kitchen, helped to serve the food, and helped cleanup. Afterwards she took us through the pantries and freezers and told us to get what we needed. We got maybe a box or two of food and was extremely grateful, not just for the food, but for the privilege to help serve.

I don't remember the time frame, but she reached out to us again out of the blue one day and said she wanted to take us shopping. So, she had us meet her at a local store that was kind of like a mini Walmart Superstore that carried everything. When we got there, we were out in the parking lot and she said for us to get whatever we want - not need - want. Her words were "act like Jesus is taking you shopping". Now we didn't know how to take this, and it was really awkward because this was totally new to us and had never happened before.

When we got inside the door we grabbed a basket and she told Belinda to get one too. One of the first end caps we come to had some snow boots for men and she asked if I had any snow boots. I hesitantly said no because I didn't want her to buy them for me, but she insisted and said "Jesus is taking you shopping today. You need boots. Here!" The awkwardness was starting to turn into a very humbling time.

As we walked through the store she would ask us if we wanted this, or that, and if we showed even the slightest interest she would put it in the basket and would say, "Jesus is taking you shopping". We were concerned of the cost adding up, but she kept on watching us, placing items in our basket. Bathing and hygiene items, bath and kitchen towels, and so on. Then we got to the food section and our baskets kept filling up. She had a basket too, but it wasn't for her as we quickly learned, and it was starting to fill up as well. We would put one thing in the basket, and she would add a few more. She would ask, "do you like this?" and if we said yes it went into the baskets. A few times she grabbed one or two extra.

About this time, we were really tearing up and getting emotional, and it was almost overwhelming. I saw a ham and she said to get one, so I picked one out. Then she looked at me and said to get another one, "Jesus is taking you shopping" is what we heard again. We got to the check out and it seemed to take forever with everything we had. I couldn't help to be curious to look at the register as I saw the total was already over $400 and we still had more to get rung up.

We barely got it all to fit in our truck and as we were saying goodbye and thanking her, she said to thank Jesus instead, and then handed us a grocery store gift card. We told her we couldn't, but she said we may need something to go with the meals that we may have forgotten. Jesus used that dear saint to take us shopping and we were blessed exceedingly abundantly above all we could ask or think. The windows of heaven opened and poured us out a blessing we were almost not able to receive. (Ref: Mal. 3:10). I know our emotions couldn't receive all the blessings from the Lord that day. We just cried in the truck before we could pull away.

We were truly favored by the Lord in Canada, and the trials came as they did, but God got us through them. Spiritual attacks don't cease when you make up your mind that you are going to follow Jesus, they can sometimes even get more intense. I have had a battle with kidney stones before in the past, and it took four days to get through it. So, as a pain rose up in my back and I got instantly ill, I knew immediately what was going on. This time we were in a foreign country with no insurance and no money, so we did what we always do when situations arise that seem to be almost hopeless. We pray, we pray, and then we pray some more. They say for men the pain can be equivalent to childbirth for women. I can believe it and can relate somewhat to that now. I didn't want to go through another long intense battle or want it to get to the point of having to go to the hospital. So, we also called a few people with unwavering faith to pray with us.

That night I couldn't get comfortable as the pain and lack of sleep was exhausting me. I did a dance of laying in the bed - switching sides - sitting in the bed - sitting in a chair - pacing the tiny apartment - drinking lots of water - going to the bathroom - getting back into bed - falling asleep for a few minutes only to go back through the same cycle. I prayed hard in the natural but mostly in the Spirit. I even prayed and laid hands on myself. It was excruciating pain, like a twisting knife in my back, and I was believing Jesus for an instant miracle.

I pleaded my case to the Lord and finally just put it all in His care. Just trusted He would come through again for me. The cycle of up, down, and pacing lasted all night long and as the sun was coming up, I finally fell asleep for many hours. When I awoke, I went to the bathroom, and when I came out I noticed the pain was gone. He did it! The battle had ended. It almost seemed surreal to be healed that quickly, but I was. In less than 24 hours and without any medical help, Jesus healed me. It was truly amazing, and I believe that was a spiritual attack on my body, as there were absolutely no side effects of the ordeal. I regained my strength instantly. God "showed up and showed out" as they say, in a huge way. It just seemed miracle after miracle was manifesting over us.

Back then, we were driving the Jimmy so much that it was already needing new tires just only after about a year and a half. I had no idea how we were going to get them, and truck tires are not as cheap as car tires. It was after a service and someone had placed an envelope in the offering with our name on it. It seemed very unusual and inside was $500 and a note that said it was for tires for the Smith's. God had spoken to the heart of someone. We had our suspicions who we thought it might have been, and once again God amazed us in a major way. Then what amazed us even more is we found out who the anonymous giver was, and it was probably the least likely person we would have guessed. So, we were able to get the new tires with that and with what someone else gave us. We never begged or solicited anyone ever. God met our needs by speaking to others.

Since then we have heard the voice of God many times over prompting us to give to someone, and when we did it obediently, we found out we met an immediate need for them. I can't count the times in the last 19 years we were blessed by someone that gave to us when we needed it the most. The many Pentecostal handshakes and provisions God gave us through someone hearing His voice. God most definitely does supply all of our needs according to His riches in glory by Christ Jesus, (Ref: Phil. 4:19), and oftentimes He uses the obedience of others to accomplish His work.

One of the last times we were with my parents in Kentucky it was found out that my dad had an inoperable brain tumor. I remember his attention span and cognize was limited, and he would sometimes just daze off and not know what was going on or who he was with. The times he was fully aware was getting less frequent I learned from my mom while in Canada.

Driving on the road traveling we'd listen to CD's, and one of my favorites was from Jimmy Swaggart. It was always so relaxing, and God's peace and presence could be felt when listening to it. Belinda said that we should make a copy of it, pray over it, and send it to my dad. So, while driving with Bishop, she got it out and we prayed, and he prayed powerfully over it. We put it in the mail with instructions for them to play it for my dad. A little later in a phone conversation with him, he said he really liked the CD and listened to it often. That it would even bring tears to his eyes.

My dad never really talked much about Godly things with me, so I really had no idea where he stood with Christ. We went to Mass as kids and he raised us in Catholic schools, but I didn't know how close he was with the Lord. But when he said the music and words would bring tears to his eyes, I knew then he felt the presence of God. Who knows? It may have been the first time in his life he ever felt His presence. I wept myself after hearing that report and praised God for touching my dad like He did. It's one thing to know God, but to feel a tangible presence that brings tears, is to really know Him.

I got a phone call that my dad was in the hospital and wasn't doing good at all, and that I should probably leave Canada immediately to see him. We booked the first flight we could get and had a stop-over in Minneapolis. In between flights I called to see how things were and I found out that he wasn't going to be with us much longer. When we got off the plane in Louisville we found out he had gone on to be with the Lord. I wished I could have gotten there in time, but then I was also relieved that he was no longer suffering. We stayed for the funeral and helped my mom through it for as long as we could but had to get back to Canada. It was hard, very hard not to be able to stay. I later found out from my mom that he used to listen to that CD all the time before he passed. I even found that same CD in their CD player five years later. One day I will see him again, and I know he is probably still singing, "Hallelujah! Praise the Lamb".

A little over a year is what we spent in Canada at that time. Even though it was very rewarding and the training we received was invaluable, we were getting anxious to either get back on the road in crusades or take a break and go home for some time. We were truly blessed to been able to have the opportunity of a lifetime to walk down this path that He laid out for us, but we were feeling it was possibly starting to come to an end after four years or so total since we first went on the road. The TV ministry was consuming much of my time as the ministry was on national TV once a week, and we also put together advertising along with TV and radio spots for teams on the road. I knew they wanted us to stay there in Canada, but I could still do my production work wherever we stayed at. We were homesick for family too.

We felt friction was stirring between us and the ministry on this matter, but we really needed to go. I'm not sure if it was our flesh, exhaustion, or the Lord directing us. The ministry gave us their blessings, but we could tell they didn't want us to leave. We had a peace with our decision after praying about it for a while. So, we headed back to Florida after stopping in Kentucky for a short visit to see my mom.

I still occasionally flew to revivals to video tape, but Belinda stayed back home to help with our third grandchild. It was an adjustment to have a place to call home again, but we were so glad we were back home. We missed the first couple of years of our second grandchild's life except for a few visits home. I think the hardest part for me when traveling on the road was not having a place to call home. I used to dread the home sections of department stores because I would get homesick and would get emotional walking through them, longing for the day when again we could buy some household items. I know it probably sounds silly to wish you could buy some kind of home furnishing, but I rejoiced and wept at the hardware store when I bought a hammer to hang some pictures on the walls. Yes, it was our walls again, and not a temporary dwelling.

Through all of our road travels, Jesus always took care of us and He still takes care of us. So, this is for you the reader too, as it is for us. When He impresses something in us, and we obey and walk in faith, it becomes His responsibility to care for us. I know I said that earlier but it's true and shouldn't be forgotten. Now don't get me wrong, we still need to do our part, but with the main responsibilities He takes over.

God told the Israelites to go into the wilderness and He sent mana down from heaven and turned the rocks into a water spicket. He told Abraham to sacrifice his son and provided a ram instead. The five thousand followed Him and He fed them. Then the same happened with the four thousand. He asked a widow woman to give her last morsel to a prophet and then sustained her. Her oil and meal basket never emptied. He called Belinda and me to another country and while there, spoke to one person and sustained us for weeks. He may be calling you to something but maybe you are fearful for provision. There is a well-respected saying and it is tried and true, "if God brings you to it, He will bring you through it". Faith walks very rarely come with a road map or a GPS directional app. But they do come with an assurance and peace that He is the navigator and provider of our journey.

Chapter 5
Coming Off The Road

I t was bittersweet the day we crossed back into the United States after the long stretch of living in Regina and helping the home church. We had met so many dear saints of God that poured into us and helped to extract out of us the gifts God blessed us with. I remember the border patrol officer asking us if we knew what day it was. "Sure", I replied. "It's Thanksgiving Day". It certainly was, and not only just on the US calendar, but in our hearts as well. We had so much to be thankful for as the last four years ignited our spirits with the mighty miracles we had seen - the numerous salvations we were in some way a part of - the spiritual training - the ministerial training - the miraculous provisions - the "hugs from God" - the friendships - the complete transformation of lives after giving themselves to Jesus… and so much more.

So yes, we knew what day it was, and we also knew that our assignment and plan God had for us was starting to come to a completion. Four plus years went by so fast, yet at times it felt like it was going in slow motion. We went from being timid followers of Jesus to bold Holy Ghost filled licensed ministers of the Gospel. That walk of faith was a spiritual boot camp, but we made it through. God showed us, no He proved that through Him ALL things were definitely possible. We were amazed at the way God chose us and used us.

The disciples in Jesus' time on this Earth were common people. I don't think a one of them ever thought Jesus would use them in the capacity that He did. None of them were seeking to be followers or leaders of the Way. He called them and as they followed, Jesus trained and taught them. Nobody had to talk them into their ministry, they just knew the Master, followed, and obeyed. One of my favorite verses about the disciples, talks about how the Sanhedrin recognized the power that transformed them from being common folk to evangelists. *"Now when they saw the boldness of Peter and John, and perceived that they were uneducated and untrained men, they marveled. And they realized that they had been with Jesus".* Acts 4:13.

Now, Peter knew who Jesus was by revelation of Him. That's why he was so quick to listen to his brother Andrew that they had found the Messiah (Ref. John 1:41). Then a little while later Jesus asked them *"But who do you say that I am?"* Simon Peter answered without hesitation and said, *"You are the Christ, the Son of the living God." Jesus answered and said to him, "Blessed are you, Simon Bar-Jonah, for flesh and blood has not revealed this to you, but My Father who is in heaven.* (Ref. Matthew 16:15-17). When we get the revelation that Jesus is the Son of the living God, we'll abandon things or ways and follow Him. It may not be to sell out completely like we did, but I guarantee there will be something we'll want to let go of that the Holy Spirit will impress upon us to drop.

Some things, or plans he calls us to may go beyond all our conventional thinking or ordered blueprint that we have in mind. But God clearly says in His word, *"My thoughts are not your thoughts, Nor are your ways My ways,"* in Isaiah 55:8. When we don't completely follow His ways and add our ways to the mix, all we get is a mess. We will have to solely depend and trust on His thoughts and ways to get to where He wants us to be.

Simon and Andrew left their fishing business along with many other disciples. Matthew walked away from his tax collecting job. James the son of Alphaeus and Judas Thaddaeus were tradesmen of some sort. Luke left his physicians practice. Paul became an outcast of the Temple... we may even become excommunicated ourselves from people, but when we get that deep rooted revelation that Jesus is the Son of the living God, we will follow Him regardless of the sacrifices He may want us to take. For the most part, His calling on our lives may not get to the point to walk away from our jobs or relocate; but He will stretch and press us out of our comfort zones to mold us into our uniquely designed purposes.

For the rest of this chapter and many other times in this book, I will be, and have been very transparent. Just yesterday we spent a good portion of the day with friends and they mentioned that they loved and respected our transparency. Anybody that tells you of all the blessings and favor, and never mentions the valley experiences are either too ashamed or proud to admit that they had testing times. But it's the testing times that forms our faith and sharpens it. Some of the testing times are brought on by ourselves by poor judgement or mistakes, while other times are ordained from Him as to test our faith. Now, tests are not designed for the instructor's benefit, but for the students. This way they can see their progress or areas they need to improve in. If we never had to endure tests in our lives, how would we know if we are learning and absorbing the material God is giving us?

As I had mentioned before, one of the main reasons we wanted to come off the road for a while is to help our daughter's family with our third grandchild that was soon to be born. Even though we were still helping the ministry with the TV, media department, and advertising; we felt it didn't warrant the ministry helping with our housing and living expenses, as we were not full-time any longer. So, we went through a very difficult transitioning in our finances.

At the time we were living in a monthly pay-as-you go converted hotel/apartment complex. The income we were taking in was not paying all the bills, so it came to a point to where we were believing God to not only meet the needs, but to get caught up as well. I was torn between going back on the road or staying home. I did fly in for a few revivals, but our truck payment started getting behind. There were also several medical bills we had been paying on for years, along with a credit card that got us in trouble as we used bad judgement on some things. Most of these were incurred before we went into the ministry. It was getting to the point to where we thought filing bankruptcy was our only option as much as we didn't want to.

The more we thought about it the more it made sense, even though it seemed somehow God wasn't helping us as much as we'd like. We weren't mad or bitter at Him, but we were puzzled as to why He would allow this as we had always been tithers and givers, and maybe felt that He owed us. But we knew that wasn't the case and that He didn't owe us a thing. He had blessed us immensely up to that time, and if He never did anything else for us besides provide salvation, that was more than enough for us.

We really prayed hard about the bankruptcy and wondered if it would damage our testimony but there was a peace about it. After all, the laws were there and in place for people in our situation, so we pursued it. We knew the consequences, that our credit history was going to be tarnished, but had the faith that God would restore everything in His timing. We placed it all in His hands, trusted that this was His plan, and that the courts would give us favor and they did.

So, everything we had on the bankruptcy was forgiven debt now. The brand new GMC Jimmy that we used for years to travel was surrendered back to the bank. The credit card account was wiped clean as well as the medical bills. Just like when Jesus first saved us, we now had a clean slate to start on. All debt had been cancelled and wiped clean. So, there we were, no debt at all. Nothing to pay back, and now we really had to depend and trust in God as we started all over with nothing but the bare basics. But we did have the wisdom learned from our past mistakes and plans to never get in that predicament again.

Now, for the first time ever we didn't have a car. When we needed to go somewhere we either walked, took the bus, or occasionally got a ride from someone. All the things we had lost could easily be replaced in the future, and I don't ever remember being sad about any of it. Actually, we were grateful that God worked things out and trusted He would restore. By this time, the section in Mark 10 when Jesus talked about giving up things for His *"sake and the Gospel's"*, and then receiving *"a hundredfold now in this time"... "and in the age to come"*, gave us great faith that this phase we were going through was just temporary.

With no bills except food and rent, we were able to save up a little to move into a different place. Where we were at, changed ownership and was turning into condos so we needed favor with a landlord, and because we had favor before, we knew God could do it again. So, after scouting around we found a place that was almost too good to be true. It was a small three bedroom, two bath, on two acres, and on a dead end road. It wasn't a fancy place, but we fell in love with it and the location.

We met with the owner and the rent was very reasonable, and he knew we were just starting over but felt to trust us. So, with favor from God, him, and the deposit from the place we were leaving, we felt we could afford this place even though we knew it would be tight. The house was full of mixed matched furniture, and even though it wasn't the nicest, we were praying it came with the house. To our pleasant surprise, the landlord said that the last tenants left it there and asked if we wanted it and if not, he would get rid of it. We graciously accepted his offer to keep it and now not only did God find us a house, but one that was furnished too.

So, we moved in almost immediately, and it was quite the change from living in a densely populated area to a quiet two acres on the end of a road. Not having a vehicle made it even more challenging. I did acquire a bicycle though, and I can still remember the other bike I found on the side of the road someone left out for trash that I took home and parts swapped. I ended up having a decent bike with wheels that didn't wobble, and a front basket to haul groceries. Two bikes that didn't cost me anything was made into one that I was so thankful for.

We were pretty far from anything around us, so the bike helped tremendously. I was still editing TV programs and had to mail one out every week. The closest FedEx drop was around 11 miles round trip on the bike, and I actually enjoyed those days. I would take two water bottles with me and space them out as the Florida heat was sweltering at times. The bike ride was relaxing, and the nature trail I road on made for a great time in prayer.

The transitioning time we were in was full of total surrender to God. Not that we hadn't done that already, but this was a deeper seeking, as the ministry was needing our help less and less since we came off the road to be with family. So, our income was becoming less, and we were really praying and believing that God was going to show us something, because we never felt a release to get outside jobs.

Our landlord had come by to check on things a few times because he had hired someone to clean up the many downed trees from the recent hurricanes that came through the past summer. The majority of the property was covered in trees except around the house. I could tell he was really getting frustrated as the person that was supposed to do the work wasn't showing up when he was supposed to, and when he did, he didn't stay long.

So, this idea came to me from the Holy Spirit, and as he was leaving one day, I felt strong to ask him something but was hesitant. I fought with it for a few minutes because I guess I was expecting a "no" answer, or that maybe he'd think it was a crazy idea, but I felt it very strong to ask. "If you can get a chainsaw, I can clean all this up for you." He looked at me and said it was a great idea and that he would get me a chainsaw and pay me the same he was paying the other guy. A few days later he came and brought it to me, and our lack of income was suddenly solved, and the tree clearing supplemented our income for several months. God did it again. He worked it out and not how we would have imagined. His plans are not our plans, and His ways are not our ways.

During this time since we didn't have a vehicle to go to church, but mostly because God was leading us, we started a home church. We got all the paperwork in order for it, and Heaven's Grace Ministry was established. Every Sunday morning, we had Sunday school, then a short service. It was mostly family attending and they brought occasional friends. Usually, there were about ten or so of us, and afterwards we would gather around the big table and have a meal. I really cherished those times, especially since we missed a lot of years when we were on the road. It was extremely hard being away from family but now here we were. We were back and had everyone together on Sunday feeding them the Word and a meal.

One of the many miracles we had at that house had to do with our lawn. Of course, we had to get a lawnmower when we first moved in but getting it to our house was going to be a challenge because we didn't have a vehicle. So, I was afraid of finding a great deal and then not being able to get it immediately and someone else getting it. I found one that was in our price range, it was self-propelled, and it had a little more power than I expected. I called the man and told him I really wanted it but didn't know when I could arrange to pick it up. I wouldn't blame him if he sold it before I could get there of course. But he asked where I lived and said he goes by our neighborhood every day and that he would bring it to us. I offered to pay him extra to deliver it, but he said no need, it wasn't a problem at all. When he brought it, it was brand new looking and was almost 2hp more than we thought we could afford. Some people would think it crazy to acknowledge something like that as a miracle, but I know God's hand of favor was on it.

I didn't mind cutting grass and Belinda would jump in and help too as we had a big yard to cut with a standard sized mower, so it took a while. We had neighbors a few doors down that we would talk to from time to time. Clare and Al were an older couple and retired, and one day she saw Belinda cutting the grass and raised some concern because it took so long to do in the Florida heat. They had just bought a brand new John Deere riding mower and offered their old Snapper riding mower to us. We insisted to pay for it, but they wouldn't hear it. It ran but needed a few minor parts to get it back in good working order and Clare even drove me to the mower shop and insisted to pay for them. We were so touched by their generosity and praised God for a very long time for this amazing blessing. God was working on our behalf and they even gave us an electric weed eater as well.

They had commented on how good of a job we had done on our yard and asked if I would be interested in cutting their properties. Yes, properties. It came to find out they owned two other houses besides theirs that they rented and were all grouped together. Probably around two acres from what I estimated, and they even said I could use their brand new mower to cut with. I said yes of course.

She always had a few extra yard things to do as well and paid me for it all. I wanted to do it for free, but she wouldn't hear of that either. God had supplemented our income again through this and really wowed us for sure. He has numerous ways to sustain us, and creative ways at that! He'll put a chainsaw in your hand and a lawn mower at your disposal and make a way out of no way. We didn't need a car at that time, our blessings came to us - right in our rented house and right in our neighborhood. We were so blessed to be able to still do some work for the ministry, have a home church, and have a great place to stay.

Clare and Al were really good neighbors. So generous and thoughtful. She had her own church she would go to and he didn't believe in church stuff much. They did know we were ministers and Al let me pray for him a couple of times as his health was getting pretty bad. I would squeeze God into a conversation occasionally but knew when to back off when I saw him start to get agitated and uncomfortable. Whenever they had to drive a long distance, like to a doctor's appointment, they would ask if I could drive them in their van. I really enjoyed those times there and the fellowship with them.

In the mornings I would go into the room of the house we used for an office, and would shut the door and pray. It was peaceful, as the only light source I had on was from the little Betta aquarium I had. Watching the beautiful blue fish swim around was relaxing, and took my focus off my work computer for the ministry and the video work I had to do. As I was praying one day

I heard the Lord Jesus speaking into my spirit. Not in an audible voice but piercing into my very being. I knew it wasn't my mind wondering or my imagination, as God was giving me specific instructions and insights into the future He had planned for us. I grabbed a little notebook and started writing down what He was giving me.

I didn't finish writing in that one sitting, it came to me over several prayer sessions. The very first thing He told me to write down besides the date of 8-28-05 was, "Don't tell anyone now" and I underlined it. That was the first thing seen when looking at it. This was the most important part of the note and a conditional instruction, and God wrote that into my heart as well. I believe I had to totally agree to that before He would release anything else, and for any of it to reach completion, I had to keep silent and commit wholeheartedly to it, and so I did. I promised Him and myself that no matter how tempted I would be to share even a portion of this note, I would hold to my promise and remain quiet until He gave the unction to speak it.

The second thing he had me write down was "pray and seek God diligently." Yes, He had me underline "diligently" too, and so I committed to that as well, not telling anyone. The third thing he had me write was a little hard to swallow, and in the flesh, I had no clue how it could happen. But He said that we were going to move back to our hometown of Louisville, KY. which I couldn't figure out why. Especially after coming off the road and settling back in Florida with our family. It was a hard pill to swallow I must say, because that meant us being separated from our family here again. But then He told me and had me write down that we were to save money for our two sons to move too. He had plans for us to bring part of our family, so I thought maybe the others were included too possibly.

So here it was the end of August and God said we were going to move after December which was four months away. I continued to seek His face on this note, and He gave me several more things to write down, one of which was a TV ministry. The last thing I wrote was similar to the first which said "don't share this with <u>anyone</u> right now. Seek Him for more direction". The next months were going to be challenging for me to keep all of this in. I normally share everything with Belinda but this time I had to walk in faith by myself and keep the note hidden in my Bible.

The Summer months and the rainy season were ending so the grass cutting job was slowing way down. I had finished all the tree clearing as well a few months prior, so our income was starting to feel it. I had pondered it for a while, but this time I felt God was saying to seek employment somewhere. The questions were where and how? All we had were bicycles for transportation now, and we were located pretty far from anything. So, my job search started, and I felt to go back into manufacturing, as I enjoyed it and had lots of experience, and thought I had a good shot at finding something nearby.

It didn't take very long to find a job, and I was hired right on the spot. I entered into a business to turn in the application and the receptionist told me to wait and the owner called me back for an interview. He asked several questions about my work related experience, and then asked about the last five years that I worked in the ministry. He knew I was a minister and mentioned the fact that most of his employees were pretty rough around the edges to put it mildly. He said there was "shop talk" language used and if I was OK with it. I think in a roundabout way he was saying this job may not be suitable for me and that I might be the sheep being fed to the wolves. But I told him that I would give it a try if he didn't mind, and how I appreciated his candidness. He kind of laughed to himself, probably thinking how interesting this was going to be having a minister work in the plant, and how it was going to play out. So, he told me to come back the next morning to start work.

Now the challenge was finding the bus or buses to get me there. I figured out there was one bus stop near our house, and it was a mile away, and the nearest bus stop to the new job was around a mile or so. Thank God the buses here in Florida have bike racks, because it would have been a lot of walking. My new schedule got me up at 4:30 am and I had to ride my bike to the bus stop to be there before 6:00. The bus ride was a good 15 miles or so, and then I rode my bike for another mile to be at work by 7:00 am. The job wasn't too bad, and I just stayed to myself a lot at breaks and lunches because the owner was right about the shop talk, but there were several there that were respectful of me being a minister, so they watched their language around me and apologized when they slipped. I wasn't pushing my faith on anyone, but I was able to talk and share encouraging words to a few there, and I hoped I made an impact somehow.

Once again I found myself climbing the ladder of promotion very quickly. The owner trusted me and really wanted me to be a shop foreman, so I was on the fast track to get that. The Bible says in Psalm 75:6-7 KJV, *"For promotion cometh neither from the east, nor from the west, nor from the south. But God is the judge: he putteth down one, and setteth up another."* God is the one that ordains promotions, and this just doesn't apply to jobs, but to ministry as well. I started there in September and by the time Christmas came around I had already gotten around $2 an hour in raises. I was now running the big machinery, was responsible for upkeep on them, and keeping production moving.

I never really made friends there, and I made a lot of them uncomfortable whenever I came around. It was some long days then and if I didn't make it to the bus stop by a certain time to get home, I would have to wait another hour before the next one came. I didn't mind too much as I got a lot of praying time in. I had a spot on the way to work that I would stop at on my bike and pray; and it took an enormous amount of praying to survive that job. It was a spiritual workout for sure and I didn't regret the extra prayer time it took.

The enemy didn't like me there and I was definitely unequally yoked and outnumbered but with Jesus, I had the advantage for sure. I stayed full of peace and joy in the Holy Ghost even though it was a constant battle in the spirit. Some days I would get exhausted, not from work, but from the spiritual battles I faced every single day while I worked there. There was a small part of me that didn't mind too much to be there, but I knew within myself because of the note, that God had a greater plan for us. I was almost on the edge of my seat everyday waiting for Him to release what he had me to write. I just kept waiting, keeping the faith in Him that He soon would fulfill his promise in that note. I didn't have a clue how He was going to do it, but I just trusted he would.

The months just kept on adding up and it was already after December, and I didn't know how much longer I would have to wait. Every workday I would pedal the bike up to the bus stop, ride the bus to my stop, pedal some more to my prayer spot, then pedal to work and face the day, work nine hours, and then head back home. It was a strange feeling knowing God had a new plan awaiting, and this plant was a steppingstone to the next one in Kentucky. As hard as it was at times, my witness there made people consider their ways and God. The pay raises carried us through, and I still did some video editing for the ministry as well.

After being without a vehicle for a year and a half our youngest son reached out to us and handed us an envelope. Inside was a signed title to a car. He immediately said the car needed work, but we were so grateful and shocked. God moved again on our behalf and used our son in the process. I got the car to a shop and all it needed was a fuel pump and we had transportation again. We weren't lacking at that time; God supplied all our needs and never forsook us. Every time we had a need He met it. I missed the bike days and the prayer stop to work, but so enjoyed again having a car. God was bringing us up and out of the bankruptcy.

Starting all over was definitely challenging to say the least but walking that walk with God by our side was a time in my life I would never change. He stuck with us - He gave us peace in the storm - as we trusted in Him He met the needs - as we struggled to get through we drew closer to Him and got to know Him more, and in a more intimate way.

Through that season and in that walk I became even more amazed how much He cares for us. Cares so much to where: He'll speak to someone to take a chance on us as a tenant when we got bad credit - supply us a furnished house - then hand us a chainsaw and pay us to clean up our own yard - put us in touch with the right person to deliver a lawn mower and buy it for a good deal - then to someone else to give us a riding lawn mower and pay for the maintenance - then hand us a key to a new mower and have a small part time lawn service - give us a bike - give us a job with promotions and raises - give us a car - brings our family to our house to have church on Sundays - press us to seek Him earnestly and consistently through a battle zone of wolves seeking to devour - sets us down and have us write a note with instructions, and then have us wait, and wait for Him to speak again so we can take the first step on a new walk of faith...

Chapter 6
The Move

S ome of the greatest times in my relationship with Jesus was when I was pressed the most from the outside. I honestly believe with everything I have that if all the bad times, trials, and tests in our lives brought us closer to Jesus, then they've served their purpose. We pray more when we are oppressed by the enemy - when we are very ill - when we have more month than we have money - when struggles are constantly before us - when we don't know the next step to take - when we're waiting for Him to fulfill a promise...

I am not saying that God gets pleasure in our bad times, or even that we should want to stay in them, but those times work together for the good so that we can move closer to Him and depend more on Him. He allows situations to hone us into a stronger person by trusting in Him. To make us, not to break us. If we never knew sorrow, we would never know true joy. If we never faced a battle, we wouldn't know the taste of victory. If we never had to endure the valley, we wouldn't be in awe of the mountain tops.

For a knife to be sharpened, it must press hard against a stone with precision to scrape off the dullness and shape it. Either we can face the hard stones and let them sharpen and shape us, or we can let them break us down. It's really a choice on our part. The plant I was working at was extremely hard with all the bad language, pokes at my beliefs, and a feeling that I had to be at the top of my witness for Him. But in the press, I prayed a lot more and not just for myself, but for the souls of those I worked with. I could have easily gotten angry or frustrated, but instead I prayed for them and their situations. It eased the tension while I was there, but it also eased my walk and peace surrounded me.

I believe God placed me there so that I would sharpen my compassion for souls and seek Him deeper than I ever had before. If I didn't pull my bike off the side of the road and pray every morning for my co-workers, the day would be stressful. The pressure I was under wasn't breaking me, it was making me. God used that job not only to sustain us financially, but to keep this warrior for the Kingdom in tip top spiritual shape and be in constant communion with Him.

We were growing so much in the Lord at that time, and we never lacked for anything. Some may look back and seen how humble we lived and maybe felt sorry for us, but it's really hard to see yourself poor when the riches of God are always abounding, and aware that He is interactive in our lives. Knowing that the same God that controls the stars and the seasons, the Creator of everything, would find time to bestow His love on us and get into every detail of our lives is beyond my comprehension. Every single step we take has His hand on it. When we serve God and trust in Him we don't live by chance or by luck, and when we can come to the full knowledge of that, we wait with anticipation for the next thing He will do.

Now, talking about the next thing He will do; Our daughter came to us and mentioned that her and her family were seriously considering moving to Kentucky and really wanted to give it a try there. They had been going through all the scenarios of how to do it, where to live, and where to work. They really longed for this and I think she told Belinda first, then Belinda told me, and asked what I thought because she felt maybe we should consider moving with them.

So, for six months I had been sitting on this note, keeping it all to myself, busting at the seams and waiting to share it with someone. Nearly every day I would pray and hold it, and read it smiling deep on the inside. No one knows how many times I pondered on it and scratched my head, yet trusting that as He said it, it would come to pass. So after biting my nails in suspense for so long, I finally got the release from God to share the note.

I remember telling Belinda to wait a second, as I had a stupid smirk on my face when I went back to the office and grabbed the note out of my Bible to show her. There were tears in my eyes and joy stirring as we read over it. There was also a peaceful release in the both of us knowing God's plan was revealed, and we were both praising Him for the awesome ways He moved. God put this together and we never had a conversation prior to this amongst ourselves, yet we all knew this was His plan. As God was speaking to me he was also speaking to our daughter. We were overcome by His presence and timing in all this, and God never ceases to amaze me - but after all, He is God, right?

Once again, Belinda and I felt to sell out all that the Lord had replaced already in the short time after coming off the road. Our daughter felt to rid a lot of their possessions too, so we arranged a "moving sale". Starting over again wasn't the most exciting thing I wanted to do, but as we had seen God's favor and provision up to this point in our lives, I had no doubt He would do it again. I believed and felt in my spirit He already had a job for me there too.

The moving sale was a huge success and we literally sold and gave away everything else that was left. We even found some people who wanted to rent the house after we moved out, which worked out great for the landlord. All that Belinda and I had left fit into the car we were blessed with. We were back to the bare basics again and His peace engulfed us as we readied for this new walk of faith, not really certain what would come next, only that we were following His lead.

I gave the plant a two week notice and let me tell you I never felt so much relief to know that my days were coming to an end there. The owner was so good to me and as anti-Christian as he was, I think I made an impact on him. He thought that job was going to break me but instead it made me stronger. I became bolder in my faith and humble before His throne, as He gave me strength to endure all this. I know God had me there as a light and as clumsy as I felt at times, I think God used me to reach a few.

The morning we left Florida to drive to Kentucky was bittersweet again as in the previous journeys. Stepping out of your comfort zone and into the Comforter's zone has its full dose of emotions for sure, but God's peace was upon us, and we knew He had us again. Everybody in our family was coming except for our youngest son, but he had plans to come at a later time. Delinda and I drove the U-Haul truck full of our daughters' stuff, and our car was on a trailer being pulled with everything we owned inside of the car. Our six month old Doberman pup Gracie, a Christmas present from the kids, was in between us in the truck cab. Everybody else was following in their van. Our daughter had an apartment lined up but nothing else much was set besides that. We were all going to have to find jobs and we were trusting in the Lord to guide our steps.

The drive was long and tiring. We were trying to make the trip in one day, but we could tell that wasn't going to happen so our kids got a hotel room for the night while Belinda, Gracie, & I took a nap in the truck. We were used to long drives and sleeping in the vehicle, as we had done it many times when on the road. We got to Louisville long before everyone else did and parked in a parking lot and had a picnic in a shady area, and I think I might have even fallen asleep for a while. I remember the sky looking so blue and we felt so much peace and prayed a lot. We had several hours to wait for everyone else to join us, and then to finally move into the apartment we were all going to share. Never would I have thought that we would move back to Kentucky, but God directed us, so I knew He was going to carry out His plan for us for sure.

After a few months our youngest son was ready to move down, so we sent after him to come. The part in the note God said to save up for our sons to move was showing now why He said that. He didn't say which way they were going to move, just that they were going to. So, our youngest moved down and then shortly thereafter our other son wanted to move back to Florida, so we helped him to move back. I had gotten a job at my brother's camera repair business and was making good money, so

Belinda and I moved into our own place. Our daughter was having a hard time finding employment and they all moved back to Florida too after trying for six months or so.

It had all seemed so crazy, and I'm not really sure what went wrong with it all, but God had spoken to Belinda and me to be there, so we were determined to stay as long as He said. Our kids were following their own paths, and as hard as it was going to be to separate from them again, we had to obey the voice of God that had me write that note, as a lot of the things still had yet to come to pass. It was heartbreaking to see them leave but God had a plan for us to pursue.

Our new landlord actually lived in Florida but rented her house in Kentucky. We had answered an ad, and she happened to be in town, so we met up with her and checked out the house. The price was very reasonable, but it needed some work, and she asked that if she bought the things it needed, if I could do the minor repairs and paint, and then she would take the money off of the rent. Sound familiar? So, this was the third time we had favor with a landlord and with our housing as God put it together. We couldn't have planned it, it wasn't coincidence, and it wasn't blind luck. I don't believe in luck and I don't think any believer should believe in luck in my opinion. You see, with God, everything happens for a purpose and on purpose for those that trust Him as their Savior. God's divine appointments seek after us when we are living for Him and put Him first in all things. So, I know it wasn't by chance that once again God placed us with the right landlord, at the right time, when there were many to choose from in a big city.

The job I had at my brother's business was really turning out to be a real blessing. I never thought I would be there long at first, and it was a field I didn't have much experience in, but I caught on quickly and learned as much as I could. So instead of this being a steppingstone to something else, it became a new career. He was needing help, I was needing work, God's timing was once again perfect.

Belinda started working at a Dollar Store as a temporary worker, but it soon turned out to be full-time, and was then promoted to assistant manager. God was proving to us once again that tithing works. He said in Malachi chapter 3 to *"prove Me"*, some translations read, *"try Me"* or *"test Me"*. Nowhere else in the Bible does God tell us to test Him. We had always been faithful to pay our tithes and He always elevated us in the workforce. Within a short amount of time after having a bankruptcy, and moving to Kentucky, we started to get on top of our finances.

We were still a one car family and my job was a good distance away, but Belinda could walk to work from where we lived. Wintertime was setting in and I use to feel bad that she would have to walk when I couldn't take her, or she couldn't get a ride. Then it happened again, someone in our family gave us a car. That was two cars in a row that was given to us. We were humbled again, and God brought us to our knees. Now, we weren't needy folk for people to feel sorry for, nor were we soliciting anyone for a handout, we just had the favor of the Lord on our side. There were two other times in our lives to where someone gave us vehicles, and this was before we came to the Lord Jesus. I don't know what the chances of getting four cars given to you in a lifetime is, but I know God was behind every single one of them. He took care of us when we first moved to Florida and was still taking care of us, and even still to this day takes care of us.

With us being settled in now, and pretty steady on our feet, we felt the leading of God to start a church, which was one of the main focuses in the note. We still had our ministerial papers with a Pentecostal organization in Canada and transferred them to the Kentucky District. We shared with them about God directing us to plant a church and how God led us thus far, and we had their support. The thing was, we had no one there in Louisville to help us. The ones that could help were already grounded in their own churches, so it was going to be just me and Belinda. The closest district church was over an hour away so help from them was going to be minimal and we knew and understood that.

We searched a few places, but nothing seemed to witness in our spirit until one day Belinda came home and said she found a church for rent. I must admit I was kind of weary because of the many other places that didn't work for us, but this one was nearby so we went to check it out. To our surprise, it was a converted warehouse space on the owner's property, fully furnished with pews and a platform. It even had a steeple on top of the building. So basically, it was pretty much move in ready except for freshening it up some with paint and a good cleaning.

The owner said they converted it for the sole use of churches, as she was a believer in Christ too, and was only going to rent it out to churches. The monthly price was very reasonable, as we had looked at other places three and four times the price of this one and wasn't as promising. So, we walked the property and prayed inside of the church, took a lot of pictures and went home to pray even more. This was going to be a huge endeavor for us because we would have to finance all of it, and we didn't even have one member yet. We were just followers of Jesus who relocated to start all over again and be dependent upon His guidance. We could have easily looked at our finances and got discouraged knowing that we were going to have to pay rent on two places, but we knew this was His will and fully trusted Him like in times past.

Jesus told His disciples to *"go"*, and as I have read in the Bible, He never told them to prepare extensively and figure everything out before acting upon His lead. Now hear me out and I know this isn't for everyone, but when Jesus sent them out two by two He told them NOT to take anything (ref: Mark 6:7-9). What?! All they had was what they had on and the power He gave them over unclean spirits. Their preparation came from faith within.

Now the power He gave after He went to the Father is even greater because He sent the Spirit in His name to live in us. Jesus said in John 14:15-17, *"If you love Me, keep My commandments. And I will pray the Father, and He will give you another Helper, that He may abide with you forever- the Spirit of truth, whom the world cannot receive, because it neither sees Him nor knows Him; but you know Him, for He dwells with you and will be in you"*. Jesus sent the Helper and He went with the disciples when they went out in twos, and then later sent the Holy Spirit again to be in them as they went into all the world after His ascension. The Holy Spirit went from being **with** them, to being **in** them, the same way He is in us today. So, if Jesus tells us to "go", rest assured the Holy Spirit goes with us because He's in us.

Jesus told Belinda and I to "go" and that's what we did. We had to look beyond the physical and pull from His Spirit that lives in us to direct us. If we did it in our way we would have never been ready or felt ready, and then when we finally did decide to go we wouldn't have needed Him for anything. Going in power and authority in Jesus takes us further than worldly preparations ever can. He can then move us, in His way, and all of our ways won't clutter up His plans. I believe many overthink the call they have on them and use preparation as an excuse to delay being obedient to the call. If God gives us the release for us to go, we are either already equipped or He will equip us along the way.

So, we prayed and really felt God saying that this was where He wanted us. The rent was manageable, and even though we were shaking in our knees in the flesh, our spirits were super excited in anticipation with what God was going to do. Our get-ahead money was now going to be used to fund a church start, but after we made the commitment, God's favor showed up in showers.

The landlord gave us the first two to three weeks free when she found out that we wanted to do some painting and such (favor once again with a landlord). We didn't have any music equipment at the time so we rented everything from a local music store, and I was afraid that our bad credit would get us a denial, but God proved me wrong, and I had to repent of my lack of faith. After we told the District we had found a place the Bishop there told us of a program they had for new churches that we knew nothing about. The way it worked is they allowed a portion of our tithes to go directly back into the church for the first year, so that covered half the rent. It was a miracle and eased up on the financial strain we thought were going to have to endure.

We got into the church and fixed it up, set up all the sound equipment, got a sign made for the outside, and then set an open date. God was moving so fast and it was humbling to think that, we, that used to run from Him in our early days, was now on the front lines in ministry serving Him in our hometown. We had a lot of family there for the first service and appreciated all their support, and knew we were definitely in His will.

All was going slow to start as far as church attendance, but we continued to push and push. A few of my nephews and their friends came to the Sunday morning services for a while and they helped us hand out flyers on a few Saturday afternoons. We advertised on bulletin boards in grocery stores, local newsletters, and then a big break happened. I was watching the local public access channel on TV one day and thought, with all our video equipment, maybe we could possibly get onto the cable channel. Actually, I know that God put the thought in me. To my surprise they had a Sunday 12:30 pm slot available, and it was free to run a program. Yes, free! Then I remembered this was on the note too. He said there was going to be a TV ministry. I had almost forgotten I penned those words down through the Spirit back in Florida over a year earlier.

That TV channel wasn't heavily watched, but it did reach a few people that came out to the services. There is really no telling how many we reached, and we always left time on the end of the program to invite the viewers to accept Jesus into their lives. My Mom watched faithfully and always made a point to compliment us on our efforts. In an encouraging email sent by her one time read, "I know it's been difficult to get your ministry going but you've made a good start and God will give you the help you need. Persistence, prayer & faith pay off and nothing worth having comes easily. Our salvation certainly didn't come easy for Jesus". I really think she was our biggest supporter and prayer covering, and something in her was changing. Even others in the family made comments how much happier she was and didn't seclude herself much anymore. The joy of the Lord was shining in her and she even made it to a few other services which was something I never thought would happen.

One day we really got touched as my Mom gave us a large donation to help with the church. I tried to refuse it and give it back to her, but she was persistent with the offering, and I never won a battle with her when it came to things like that. We used it for advertising and many other things. Somebody else in our family gave to us which went towards a lighted marquee sign that we put in front of the church close to the road. Every week I would put an encouraging word or scripture on it so the traffic that rode by would see, but the growth of the church was slow going and just wouldn't take off.

With three services a week and holding down full time jobs, Belinda & I didn't have a lot of spare time to put the efforts in like we wanted to. There were many services that it was only three of us there including Jesus, but we praised Him like it was a full house no matter. Sometimes I would just preach to the video camera for the TV programs we produced. I know it may have sounded ridiculous to have a service with no one there, but we did it anyway. Then there were other times if nobody showed up we would just have a song service and just pray.

Occasionally, I would talk to the landlord's husband as he would come in and visit for a little while when we would be there cleaning up or cutting the lawn. He never would come into a service, nor did he attend his wife's church routinely. He loved and believed in God, just wasn't a church goer for some reason. One day while talking to him I came to learn that he would sit outside the church and just listen. He said he really liked the worship and preaching we did. I had no idea, and after I found out I was elated to know that the times we still held a service when no one was there, we actually did have someone listening in and getting ministered to. We could have easily just waited to see if anybody was going to show up and just left, but God had us to press onward, and there was a couple of times that we had some late comers, so it was a very good thing we pressed through.

We had the church for a year or so now and we were all shocked when my Mom had passed in her sleep. She looked very peaceful when my oldest brother found her. Myself and my brother I worked for went over to the house immediately and she was positioned like she was ready to get out of bed. The covers were halfway pulled off and it looked like she was ready to swing her feet off the bed. I really believe she was seeing Jesus and was starting to get up to meet Him when He called her home. It was hard and totally unexpected, but we were so grateful she transitioned so peacefully. She was with Jesus now and my dad.

From that point going forward the church just didn't feel the same. Belinda and I both felt a closure, and even though our last push in the church was successful with a new family attending, we knew it was coming to an end. It was as if my Mom's prayers were the glue that held everything together and now that she was gone, so was her prayer covering. We tried to hang onto the church for a few more months, but it just felt like God was telling us that it was OK to close the doors for good.

It was a very difficult decision, and there was a part of me that felt like I had failed Him. We were doing this for a year and a half now and it was going nothing like we had imagined in our minds. Sometimes, when no one showed up I would just stand outside the church doors and wave at the cars that drove by and would pray, "Lord, I pray that You would bless them, and that they would come to the knowledge of Your saving grace". Some people waved back, some honked their horns, and many would just give a blank stare. My heart ached and I thought about all the eyes that were watching us - our family there in Kentucky - family in Florida - the District office - the TV audience - the few that would come occasionally - our landlord - her husband... I know we could have tried harder and pushed more, but we were at the point of exhaustion. Then Belinda reminded me that if we were only there for a few or even one person, it was worth it all. We both agree now that my Mom was the main one, and that's why we felt closure after she passed.

To be a part of God's plan and not see the reasoning behind it all until you see the backside of it takes one's breath away. God doesn't always reveal the purpose of a plan from the beginning, He just wants us to be obedient to his leadings. If God said that we were going to move back to Kentucky to start a church to be able to reach my Mom, I might have been like Sarah in Genesis 18 and laughed when I heard it. The Lord told Sarah she was going to have a child when she was well past the age of childbearing, and I probably would have also doubted that God could break through all the religious traditions and teachings that my Mom believed in all her life had God given me the heads up.

The Lord asked Abraham, *"is anything too hard for the Lord?"* (Ref. Gen. 18:14). If we were to have a conversation with Him and question the plan(s) for our lives, I am sure He would ask us the same thing. I am not sure if my Mom ever left her religious background, and that really doesn't matter, but I do know she drew closer to Him. She became happier, and the bitterness she held onto was dropped and replaced by His joy.

As much as we felt unworthy, unready, uneducated, untrained and inexperienced to pastor a church, we did it anyway. We would have missed God's timing otherwise if we would have waited to feel ready. The truth of the matter is, and this spreads across a large spectrum, is that not everybody God calls answers the call, or they delay it trying to get into the mold the church world has formed. God is telling them "go", and they are not knowingly saying "no". There are many that are anointed, trained, educated, held at high reverence amongst their peers... but if God would tell them to drop everything to move and start over from scratch, they would laugh. Not because of lack of faith in themselves, but lack of faith in Him. Because the world does it one way, and they think God would do it in the same way for them. But nothing is too hard for the Lord!

As I was saying before, I felt like I failed in the world's eyes by closing the church, but also felt we accomplished God's purpose behind the plan and had a peace about it all. Beyond a shadow of a doubt, I know we were in His perfect timing. Yes, there are some things I would have done different - some things I regret - some things we fumbled through - but we took away so much with us by stepping out of our comfort zones. I am sure people were shaking their heads trying to rationalize our efforts, but it didn't matter. We obeyed God and there were a few people that we made an impact on for His Kingdom.

When our walks of faith abandon all premade ideas, then after we muddle through the criticisms and judgements and all we are left with is the consequences of our decisions; we can then know that it was better *"to obey God rather than men"* (Ref. Acts 5:29), and walk with our heads held high and hold a clean conscience before Him and ourselves.

Chapter 7
The Lonely Walk

W ith my Mom passing and the closing of the church, there came an emptiness inside that maybe God was done using me and now we were left to somehow redeem our standing in the ministerial world. We were so bold and sure that God was going to build the church at the beginning, and that we were going to grow out of that space we rented. But growth never happened, and as much as I tried to beat myself up over closing the doors, Belinda kept on reminding me that if we were there for just one soul, it was worth it all. There were many times on the road in services that only one person came to the altar to accept Jesus, and we believed that all the efforts and expenses of holding the meetings was worth every bit of it. *"Let him know that he who turns a sinner from the error of his way will save a soul from death..."* is what it says in James 5:20.

Some churches are number counters and feel that if only just a few people come to the altar, they are not very effective and hang their heads low. What if they celebrated just one person coming to Jesus just as much as if it was one hundred? Jesus gave us the parable of the shepherd that left the ninety-nine to go after the one that was lost. The shepherd had to stop what he was doing to go after the stray and left the others to do so. If those sheep could talk, they were probably saying that their shepherd was crazy to waste all his time to go after the lone one.

Or maybe they were cheering him on because they had compassion too. Regardless, the one was worth value and the shepherd considered not himself to go after it.

The Bible says that he went to the mountains and carried the sheep back down rejoicing (Ref. Mat. 18:12-13, Luke 15:4-7). The mountains can be a treacherous place with steep cliffs and sharp rocks. It would be easy to lose footing and trip, or even fall but he went anyway. Even though it would have been easier to just not think about it, and let the risk outweigh the effort; his conscience wouldn't let him forget about the one though, because it was in his power to go and seek. He would rather travel the path of sacrifice instead of trudging the road of regret.

It was strange not to stop by the church any longer on my way to work which I had done almost daily. I would just walk around the inside the church and pray. Sometimes I would just sit in a pew or sit on the platform and pray, maybe play the keyboards, worship... That had been my norm for over a year and a half now. I would spend lots of time preparing for Wednesday night's service, Sunday morning's service, and Sunday night's service. Seemed like most of my time was consumed with preparing messages. Now I was waiting in the land of "what's next?" Sunday mornings were the worst for me, right at the 11am service time I would look at the clock and just breakdown weeping. I was being torn up inside between what I lost and possibly what could have been. I was mourning the loss of the church yet had a peace that we did the right thing.

To my shocking surprise my Mom and Dad left us six brothers an inheritance that helped Belinda and I with a down payment to buy a brand new house. Yes, brand new. We didn't qualify for anything but new housing as we were still rebuilding our credit rating from the bankruptcy. They say it takes like seven years to get back on top from bad credit, but only about three years had passed, and God was doing it much quicker. We had lost our new truck, a car, and our house; we also moved a couple of times since then, but God was giving us His favor. We had never missed paying our tithes or giving offerings, and I know God was honoring us. Not only was He giving back what the devil stole from us but was making him pay it back with interest.

The next months were exciting as I was at the new house almost daily to walk the two dogs now, and to see the progress of our house being built. We had the perfect location at the end of a dead-end road, with no neighbors to one side of us, only a wildlife preserve. This kept my mind occupied and busy, as I avoided thinking about missing the church. Our house was the very first one built there, and I was praising God for His goodness and love He graciously gave us. I remember again in His Word where He said he would give us houses and lands in this time, to those that left them for His sakes and the gospel's. (Ref. Mark 10:29-31). I felt I didn't deserve a brand-new house, but He did say whatever we sowed that is what we are going to reap. We could have abandoned our travels on the road years earlier to try to save our old house, but instead we put it in God's hand and let it go. Some might think that was a hard decision, but God's peace over it made it really easy. I believed His Word, but seeing it built right before my eyes took on a whole new meaning and love for Him. We weren't boastful, but thankful.

Closing day on the house finally came and the upgrades we made were beyond my expectations not in looks, but at the fact that we could afford them. When choosing cabinets, counter tops, flooring, exterior features, and even the energy efficient windows and furnace, we made it a point to get what we wanted. We thought this was where we were going to retire so we spared no expense. We also had hopes to possibly one day start another church after we got settled in. It was almost a dream come true and we humbly thanked God for shining His face upon us numerous times over. The new fence went up, the appliances were delivered, and new furniture started to be bought. We both had good paying jobs, and without having to help fund a church, for the first time in a long time we had extra money.

The cars we were driving were finally going to be replaced. My '88 Lincoln Town Car sure was a blessing, but the rear end was starting to go out and no A/C made it miserable at times. It was a good car and I am still thankful to our son for giving it to us, and also for my Mom helping with some repair costs. I think I had that car for almost two years, and we ended up getting a slightly used Ford Focus wagon, and that car worked out beautifully for our needs. A short time later it came time to replace Belinda's car and she really wanted this little red Chevy Aveo she kept looking at online at the used car place. She viewed it many times over for weeks, and it was like God was holding it there for her, as she knew it was her car. So, we went a got it, and was able to manage a large down payment for it.

I was even so blessed to have the resources to replace my musical instruments that I sold when we first went on the road some six or seven years prior. I had already replaced my acoustic guitar when we had the church, but I now had an electric guitar and amp, bass guitar, and even some inexpensive electronic drums along with some other PA equipment. Belinda cried more than I did when I had to let the original music equipment go when we first started on the road, but now I was crying probably more than her just looking at the way God made a way for me to have them back in my life.

I once again pondered on the verses in Mark 10:28-30 when Peter said to Jesus, *"See, we have left all and followed you."* Jesus assured him that anyone that gives up something of value in this life will be repaid in this life. Not necessarily in the same way, and more than likely with persecutions, but I was seeing God restoring back to us miraculously what we unselfishly had given up.

Not only just the music equipment, but many other things: we had to sell our first house, now we were in a brand new one - we gave away new furniture and appliances to go on the road, now we had new ones - we lost two vehicles in the bankruptcy, now we were buying newer ones... We were overwhelmed with God's blessings yet there was still a part of us that was empty. We missed being on the road and having our own church. Financially we were thriving, but spiritually we were drying up.

We were visiting churches on Sunday's and had not really found anywhere we could call home. I think one of the hardest parts of moving to a new city is finding a church. I know some find one quickly and are locked in with very little effort, but with us, to find something that was similar to our ministerial training seemed almost rare. We did find a church nearby that had a love for Jesus like we did, and I assimilated right on in with them. The pastor never really had to ask about our credentials, nor did we have a lengthy conversation about our background, we just knew that God brought us together. It didn't take long at all and I started helping on their music team playing acoustic guitar and occasionally leading a song or two. I would preach a couple times a month as well for them and never really expected anything in return, I just loved serving the Lord there and being used again for His Kingdom.

After six months or so, our suspicions became confirmed that there were some doctrinal differences between us. We were rooted and grounded in our beliefs, and I never was constrained when I preached for them, but there came a day when they were planning a baptism for several new converts there. The pastor was announcing it and made a comment that after they got baptized, they would be saved. Now we were taught, and firmly believe, that baptism is not part of salvation, but they believed it was. I had never really run into a situation like this before, nor did I know what to do. We had invested a lot of time, and I had invested so much of myself into this church. To us, this was our church too and our home. Our tithes were going there, and we even helped financially with the building fund. We also found out too that they didn't believe in the Trinity. We believe that God manifests Himself as the Father, Son, and Holy Spirit, but they were what some refer to as a "Jesus Only" church.

Belinda asked the pastor several times if they had a statement of faith and he would just comment that they believed like we did and loved Jesus. I mean our beliefs were almost identical except for these two major things. It almost seemed like they were hiding this from us, either intentionally or not I'm not sure, but we knew we could no longer fellowship there any longer. This was almost a shock to me that they didn't believe in the triune of God, and that they really believed these new converts weren't going to be saved until they got baptized.

I got to know a few of the members, and I could tell God transformed their lives. It was sad that they really thought they weren't saved until they undergone a baptism ritual. I mean to have the love of Jesus inside of you and to feel that you weren't saved? That's not the way God intended it. John addresses both of these saying, *"For there are three that bear witness in heaven: the Father, the Word, and the Holy Spirit; and these three are one"*. 1 John 5:7. Then says, *"And this is the testimony: that God has given us eternal life, and this life is in His Son"*. 1 John 5:11. Nowhere have I read that baptism is essential for salvation, but that it is an act of obedience. Yes, Jesus said *"He who believes and is baptized will be saved; but he who does not believe will be condemned"*. Mark 16:16; but He never said or implied that not getting baptized will condemn us, only not believing.

So, as painful as it was, we had to part our ways with this church. I am not sure if God hid these differences from us for a season, or we were just that blind not to see them because we were hungry to serve. There were many there that we got to minister to though, and I pray we made a difference in their lives. If we were there just for that, it was worth it all. I had one man come up to me after a service, (I preached about being filled with the Holy Spirit), and he said he tried so many times to receive Him, but never succeeded. He longed for God's Spirit to fill him, but it seemed like there was a roadblock. I looked at him and with wisdom from God told him, "to be filled with the Spirit of God, first you have to empty yourself of self". He looked at me and I saw he was taken back with what I said. I could tell no one ever told him that before, and he really considered it. That maybe there was something in his life that he couldn't let go of that was keeping him from being filled with God's Spirit. I am not sure if he ever pressed his way through, but I am glad I was there for him.

At the time, our young grandsons were living with us temporarily because our daughter was considering moving back to Louisville, so we were helping her out. I used to bring them to church with me and I could tell they enjoyed it. One service there after I got done preaching, I gave an altar call for people to receive Jesus as their Savior as I always do, and my youngest grandson came to the front. Immediately the tears started flowing from my eyes and when everybody else saw it, the tears were flowing in that place. That was eleven years ago, and the seed that was planted was worth every bit of our efforts in that church. We may have been used and abused, (that pastor never reached out to us after that), but if God allowed it all so I could impact a few, I gladly accept the heartbreak of it all. Jesus said that He came to heal the broken in heart, and I know He knows about that, as His disciples all fled the night He was betrayed. So even though that walk of faith ended and knocked the wind out of me for quite a while, Jesus came in and healed this broken heart.

"He heals the brokenhearted and binds up their wounds".
Psalm 147:3

"The Spirit of the LORD is upon Me, because He has anointed Me to preach the gospel to the poor; He has sent Me to heal the brokenhearted, to proclaim liberty to the captives and recovery of sight to the blind, to set at liberty those who are oppressed; to proclaim the acceptable year of the LORD." Luke 4:18-19

After we closed down our church, I thought about how God was done with me, but He showed me at the church we just left, that He still wanted to use me. But once again, we were left with trying to figure out our "what next?". I couldn't understand why there seemed to be a trend going of these short windows in ministry. All we wanted was a place to call home and feel like we landed.

I used to work with a man when I was in my late teens that flew small, single engine airplanes as a hobby. He would rent one, fly to a city just to eat a meal, and fly back. He asked me to go with him one time, but I never took him up on the offer, as I was on a small plane before and didn't like it much. He was explaining to me that sometimes he wouldn't really go anywhere but would practice, (I think it may have even been a requirement to keep his pilot's license), "touch-and-go landings". This is when you would come in for a landing, touch the wheels to the ground, and then take back off into the air. I was starting to feel like that is what our ministry life was becoming. A series of "touch-and-go landings", and never really parking in a hanger and turning the engines off. As soon as we would touch our wheels to the ground and roll for a while, God would tell us to pull back up.

This time it shook me up bad. I felt like such a hypocrite to everyone I knew to pull away from a church that I had so enthusiastically gave of myself to serve. I mean it wasn't like we just went to visit and be benchwarmers, but we had our feet in the trenches - working the altars - preaching - helping with outreach - helping outside of church hours - participating in music practice and the worship team. Church just wasn't a Sunday thing; it was a lifestyle.

Belinda worked a lot of weekends with her job, but I was always off, so I spent a lot of time alone then. I would sit around and cry out to God my afflictions of why He would gift me with so many things, and then just have me sit on them. At times, the loneliness was unbearable, and I would just weep uncontrollably trying to figure out what I could have done different, or where it went wrong. I never could pinpoint it directly to any one thing, and the agony of having God's fire inside of me with nowhere to release it was putting me in a state of deep, dark depression.

During this time, I started a journal to write down my thoughts, feelings, and lessons learned from the Lord. Now, I didn't just want to make it through trials, I wanted to be strengthened by them, so I wrote them down. As I was struggling through all of this, I did a lot of seeking, praying, and fasting with hopes that He would speak to me. This is the very first entry and my thoughts. He wasn't just speaking to me, but to both of us:

"We have to give to God (surrender) our wants, our dreams, our preconceived ideas of what we think He wants us to do. As hard as it may be, we have to give Him our past ideas of what we think He wants us to do and start over. His ways and thoughts are higher than ours. Somewhere we missed direction and guidance so we must start over from scratch. For Him to reveal we must

totally open our eyes and ears and not limit or be blind to what He has for us.
Can't put new wine into old bottles. Can't put new cloth on an old garment".

Now that's what I was feeling at that time. That maybe we missed something. That it was our fault. But after living life a little bit longer and ten or so years have passed now, I can see it was actually part of God's plan. It's said that, "hindsight is 20/20", and if I knew it was His plan to go through that time in ministry, I probably would have not slipped so deeply into depression. I probably would have gotten up exponentially faster, but God was working on my faith and I had to travel down that road.

I knew I had to do something, and Belinda came across some information about a new social media tool called Blog Talk Radio to where you could have your own internet radio program, and the plans started for free. So, we prayed about it and God spoke to me to start a live nightly broadcast and call it, "15 Minute Devotion". We also upgraded to the premium package so we could take live phone calls for prayer. We would almost tag team on the air, and did that for a few months, but it was hard to get a following so we canceled the broadcast.

It did feel good to have a ministry purpose for a while and then I started falling into a deeper state of depression. We had lunch with our Bishop over the District one day, and even he could sense it as much as I tried to play off as being "OK". I remember him praying for us before we left and his words coming against oppression on me. I thought it kind of strange as I never had someone pray for me in that way with the word "oppression", and it felt like a rebuke in a way.

It impacted me so much that I went home and almost immediately started doing research on oppression. Jesus had come in and healed my broken heart from being used at that last church, now I was believing for Him to, *"set at liberty those who are oppressed..."* (Ref. Luke 4:18). "Oppression" is defined as "a sense of being weighed down", and that's exactly how it felt. It felt like something was pushing/forcing me down and a heaviness was on top of me, almost smothering.

Now, depression comes from the inside, but oppression comes from the outside. Yes, I was feeling sad and lonely which were feelings from within, but I came to the revelation that the devil was oppressing me, which was coming from without. He was heavily weighing me down with guilt, worthlessness, and hopelessness. You see oppression also means, "prolonged cruel or unjust treatment or control". All that time, yes I fought with having the blues, but when I realized that some, if not all of what I was sensing, was the enemy trying to forcibly hold me down, and take all the fight out of me and give up for good, I felt hope once again.

Other Bible translations for Luke 4:18 uses the word *"bruised"* instead of *"oppressed".* Bruising just doesn't happen by someone wishing affliction on you, but there is a point of physical or spiritual contact. Being that, *"we do not wrestle against flesh and blood, but against principalities, against powers, against the rulers of the darkness of this age, against spiritual hosts of wickedness in the heavenly places"*, Ephesians 6:12, this bruising is not physical, but spiritual then.

Bruising hurts - it leaves marks and whelps - it changes your appearance. "A bruise is always caused by internal bleeding into the interstitial tissues which does not break through the skin, usually initiated by blunt trauma", (Wikipedia). This is why I said earlier that oppression comes from the outside. For me to feel the way I did meant that I had been afflicted, (beaten up spiritually you could say). So that meant I could be healed, and Jesus came to free those oppressed or bruised. Hallelujah!!!

I had made up my mind...this was NOT it! I could accept that maybe I was hurt and was healing from the inside, but when I knew that this oppression was forced upon me, it almost infuriated me. I was like, "how dare you devil come down on me and exercise unjust treatment!!! I am a child of the King and I refuse to be treated like this any longer"! So, I started pulling out some resources with Christian books on turning things around, and instead of wallowing in despair, I started praising Him with singing and music. It was a gradual process for sure, but I was digging my way out now.

I know that Belinda's prayers were impactful too, probably more than anything else, but I felt bad that I was supposed to be this strong spiritual leader and yet I was fighting and grasping for peace. I can now understand how some can fall into despair and not try or want to get out of it. It's because the weight of the oppression gets easier to carry than the effort, or force it takes to get out from under it. We'd much rather carry it and learn how to cope, rather than exerting all we got to break free. But Jesus never meant for us to do it by ourselves, He said He was sent to set free those that are oppressed.

I used to walk the house rebuking the devil almost in a rage against this oppression over me; sometimes shouting and straining my voice, and then other times I would be going through a box of Kleenex in one prayer sitting, quietly pouring myself out before Him. I wrote a song which was birthed in my agony through all this and in the chorus, it says:

> *"Holy Spirit rescue me.*
> *This flesh is fighting battles set me free.*
> *A reflection of your image is what I want to be.*
> *It's what I long to be.*
> *It's what I need to be".*

During this time of darkness over my life, I turned to God a lot more instead of pulling away. Now don't get me wrong, there were a few times in my despair I had choice words with Him, but I quickly repented knowing that He was ultimately in control. This brought me closer to Him more than I ever experienced before. I said it before, but I'll say it again, that if all the bad times in our lives brought us closer to God, then they served their purpose; and I'd like to add, that when I was hurting and oppressed the most, is when He was holding me the most.

God will show us things so we can act upon them. He showed me that I wasn't only going through severe depression, but I was being attacked by oppression from the enemy. He then, through a journey of hurts, strengthened me to overcome. He could have delivered me instantly I suppose, but the wealth of knowledge I learned through the process was invaluable. I would have never traded it for the easier way out. I now recognize when oppression is being forced upon me, and I quickly rebuke it and shun it away.

I believe there are many Christians that are swimming in a sea of oppression that has been disguised by the devil as depression. He has tricked them into thinking something is wrong with them, but really, he has only stripped them of their power in God by manipulation. He has forcefully held them down to prevent them from getting back up and lied to them and told them they were depressed. We don't need to long to feel better, we need to pick up our Sword which is the Word of God and take back our territory - take back our peace - take back the plans He has for us - take back our lives in the name of Jesus!

Chapter 8
Uprooted

A s I was finally breaking free from the holds of the enemy, I was looking into serving somewhere so I started viewing through the ads. Not that I am in the habit of doing such a thing, but I just didn't know where else to turn. I wasn't seeking for a church per say, but just for the opportunity to use my music talents for the Kingdom. My heart was wanting to be a blessing and meet some brethren. So, I came across an ad for Christian musicians, and this church was needing a drummer and a guitar player, so I inquired. I met with the worship leader, and we felt an immediate connection, so the next time they had music practice I brought my guitars. I had also met the Pastor of the church during that time and we started attending there for a while. The band was playing more contemporary worship while at the church it was more Southern Gospel style.

They were into music that had guitar or steel guitar solos every so often, but it didn't quite sit with my spirit. Even though I came from a rock music background before I got saved and played lead guitar, I felt it turned the spotlight towards man and away from God. I felt very awkward when they would motion to me to go into a guitar solo, I would pass sometimes but other times I would do it just to appease them. When they knew that I could play lead really well they encouraged me to do it more often, but on the inside, I was perfectly content praising Him with just rhythm strumming.

I can't put it into words, and I don't condone worship teams having solos, but for me, it felt like I was taking the spotlight and God was taking a backseat. So, after a little while of being there I pulled myself away from them. I know I hurt the worship leader as he had plans to take the band out into the community for outreach, but I had to follow my convictions. I explained where I stood but we didn't see eye to eye, and it kind of ended bitterly.

I wasn't being disrespectful to them, but when I got saved, I was impressed hard by God about the music we listened to prior to our conversion in Christ. At that time Belinda and I took all the rock music CD's we had, roughly around two hundred, and went to the pawn shop to unload them. We walked away from music that glorified people and man, so we could transition over to music that exalted God. It was our conviction, and I don't think many can understand it, but as I look back with no regrets, I still to this day shun away from music or musicians that take the stage away from the One that gave them their talent to begin with.

So there I was, left again with nowhere to serve in ministry and no home church. I was also left with the feeling that maybe something was wrong with me, but I realize now that not all callings are the same. Maybe God brought me to that church long enough to show them that they weren't worshipping Him as they should and lost their focus. Only God really knows.

Around the same time, Belinda was having really bad problems in her right knee, and had been going to the doctor frequently to have fluid drained off of it. It would swell up so big all the way down into her foot, and especially after working all day. Just when we thought maybe it was getting better it would get worse again. It got so bad that it looked like the only option was a knee replacement. She was maxed out with the amount of shots she could have for it, and the swelling was out of control. She was at the doctor's office weekly now to get it drained.

So, we scheduled the surgery and got it done, but there was major complications and she had to go back a week later for a second surgery. The week in between was probably the worst week of her life as the pain was so intense that no number of painkillers would take off the edge. If there was one week in our lives that we could erase, that would be the one. There is so much more to this story, but the truth is the devil wanted her dead but did not prevail. So finally, after the second surgery she was able to start physical therapy all over again. She was out of work for quite some time, but God sustained us and made a way for her to return. The months of suffering with her knee had finally came to an end and recovery was looking great.

Shortly after all of that our youngest son made an announcement that he was getting married and asked me if I would officiate the wedding. I was thrilled that they asked, and considered it an honor, so we had to make plans for a road trip to Florida. Leading up to all this, being separated from our family was taking a toll on us, and especially with Belinda. The time we spent on the road and seeing her almost in anguish was prevalent again, and we knew there was no way we could stay in this brand new house and retire here with our family nine hundred miles away. So, we made the decision to put the house up for sale just to see what would happen. We said, "if it is God's will, He will make it happen". There was really nothing holding us there in Kentucky except for that house. Well, our jobs of course too, but He has always been faithful to provide them for us, so we had no doubt we would find new ones.

We listed the house with a Buy Owner company that helps you sell your house with no realtor. It sounded great. No commissions to pay, but we soon found out that our four hundred dollars we spent to list our house was a waste of money, as we didn't even get one inquiry over a three-month period. We could have looked at that as a sign that maybe we were to stay, but we were really starting to feel strong that it was God's will for us to move back to Florida. He even spoke into my spirit the city "Winter Garden", which is just west of Orlando. So, we prayed hard for God to make a way for us to sell our house and move. Belinda had mentioned she knew a realtor lady from her job that would come in occasionally, so she asked her to come out to the house and see what she thought.

Now during this time, the housing market was at a low and houses just weren't selling. The realtor came out and walked the house and we started talking about spiritual things and how we were ministers, which sparked a conversation about the loss of her daughter. She talked for a long time, about her walk with the Lord when she was younger too. When she started talking business, we got the impression that she was going to sell our house for us and take very little commission, (she made a comment to that effect), and because she knew Belinda pretty well from their conversations at her job.

We felt it such a blessing and it looked like our move back to Florida was really going to happen now. We weren't just testing the waters but was all-in now and signed the contract with the realtor. I must say at first, I was sorting through my feelings about selling our dream house and starting all over again. We had started over many times now and it was really getting old as I hate moving, but God's peace was all over us. Even though the market was slow, we had faith God was going to do it. He's never let us down before and this time was no different.

A couple of weeks after we put the house up for sale, we were driving to Florida for our son's wedding and on our way down we got a phone call from our realtor that someone had put a bid on the house. The offer was quite lower than the asking price and I was almost insulted and got mad. We would have lost money if we accepted the offer. She said she would talk to the potential buyer and would try to get a more sensible offer, as even she was floored with the low bid. She knew we would say no but had to appease the buyer even after she strongly advised them it was a bad idea. She also mentioned they were hard to deal with.

So, we continued driving and it took a while for me to shake off the lowball offer, but when we were crossing into Florida I saw the welcome sign. As I was looking at it and saw all the palm trees lining the highway, I remember getting overcome, and a sense of peace was consuming me telling me that we were home. I also felt an instant disconnection with Kentucky and that drive into Florida eased my spirit and sparked hope once again.

I then knew God had a new plan for us as we entered through the door at that border line.

I can't remember if I shared it with Belinda right away, but I held back the emotions as best I could just knowing Florida was our home again. When we did talk about it, I told her, "it feels like we are home", and felt an easiness in my spirit. There was also something about Winter Garden that God put into me that was in the background of my thoughts.

Now the last five years or so in Kentucky was coming to an end. We were so deeply rooted there, and I really thought that was our home. God led us there for a reason and for a season, but He had another plan as we were learning. My family there thought we were crazy when I mentioned we were considering moving back to Florida. We had a brand new house - we were settled - had really good jobs - cars that were only just a few years old... but now no peace in staying there.

God miraculously got us all to Kentucky years earlier and everyone but us went back to Florida. We believed they might return again, and some did for a while, but Florida was home to all of us. That's where the kids were raised for most of their youth, and that's where Belinda and I started our lives together and got married. Our time in Kentucky almost seemed surreal as it was ending. God gave me that note to get there and almost all of it came to pass with the church - the TV ministry - how our sons moved there - how some of our family would be a part of the church. Even though the outcome of everything didn't turn out like I thought it would, God never said everything was going to be permanent, only that it was going to take place.

The wedding was fantastic, but we wished we could have stayed longer, and we gladly welcomed our new daughter-in-law and her family into ours. With me officiating the wedding just blessed my soul even more than I can express, and the feeling that Florida was going to be our home again brought tears of joy. While we were there at our daughter's place, they made a comment that the apartment unit right below them was available for rent. We kind of dismissed the idea right away being that we had two Doberman's and needed a backyard. It seemed very impractical, but a great idea, nonetheless.

We couldn't stay in town long for the wedding, as we had our jobs to get back to and had family dog-sitting for us. We basically drove to Florida and had to turn right back around and head back to Kentucky. The drive there and back gave us lots of time to talk, and how we knew we were doing the right thing by selling the house and moving. Possessions are replaceable but family isn't. We longed to be back with them, and God was honoring our heart's desire.

We got another call from our realtor after we made it back and she said the same potential buyer we shunned away and shook our heads about, came back with another offer and we needed to see it. I was extremely skeptical and was thinking this was going to be a waste of time and an insult to us again, but to our surprise and by God's grace, he offered almost exactly what we were asking. I am not sure what changed on his end, but it was amazing that we were selling our house to the first person interested in it, in what the media was calling a dead housing market. We accepted the offer and God heard our prayers, and we were now on our way back "home". He was moving so fast and I must say I was emotional as we were getting ready to close this walk of faith and go on another one. Our time in Kentucky led us from faith to faith and made me stronger in Him. He used the darkest, loneliness time in my life to draw me closer and trust Him more.

Now we were left with the task of scaling down again. We had acquired so many things, especially from my parent's estate. We knew we couldn't take everything and immediately started to put things up for sale. They were selling so quickly at the prices we were wanting. I was once again amazed at God's hand over our situation, so much that He would take my breath away with His faithfulness and goodness. God was working it out, and faster than I ever anticipated. What seemed impossible with man was possible; and even today, the impossible is still possible with God. I can't even count the times He has proven this to me.

The weeks were counting down and we were getting nearer to the closing date when our female Doberman, Gracie, started to get really sick. We've noticed she was getting less energetic than she used to be over the last little while. Then she started throwing up what looked like coffee grinds, which we learned was dried blood, and we immediately rushed her to the vet. They did some testing and sent her back home after ministering barium, so that we could bring her back later for a CT scan.

Apparently, she had some kind of intestinal blockage and we were really concerned, as she was only five years old. Belinda was going to wait until the medicine fully kicked in and take her back to the vet for the scan. I had to go back to work to finish the rest of the day, as I couldn't really take off then. The barium didn't pass through all of her intestines, so the vet said there needed to be an emergency surgery. We consented, and then we got a phone call that we needed to go back to the vet immediately. I remember leaving work and on the drive home I was in tears most of the way. I don't know how I saw the road with all the emotions running down my face. That was our Gracie girl. Everybody loved her and she loved everybody. All I could think and pray about was for God not to let her die on our granddaughter's birthday, which was that same day.

When we got there the doctor said he had found numerous tumors in her intestines and bowels, and said they could possibly remove them, but they would also have to remove a few feet of her lower intestines as well. He really didn't think her outcome was going to be good if she survived the surgery, and the recovery time would take months even if it was successful. The odds were extremely low, and we had to make one of the hardest decisions in almost a moment's notice and decided it would be best to put her to sleep. It was tragic as it all happened so suddenly. It was to say the least, heartrending.

It was hard to carry on, but we only had about two weeks before the closing of our house. God was working out everything including where we were going to stay in Florida. Our son-in law was in apartment management and the unit right below theirs was still available. That same place we dismissed so quickly as a possibility to live seemed more manageable and ideal now with only one Doberman. So, he put it together for us and the price was surprisingly very affordable. Talk about favor, not only were we moving, but staying right below part of our family was God for sure. We didn't even have jobs lined up yet and we got favor with the apartment rental company on the lease, and it was okay to for Buddy our surviving Doberman to stay there too.

Everything was falling into place and carefully orchestrated by God. He was doing it again for us. It wasn't okay that Gracie had cancer and had to be put to sleep, but the timing seemed to be perfect. If she would have not taken ill so quick, we would not have moved into that apartment. But God knew, and as much as it hurt to lose her the way we did, peace surrounded us.

I worked part of the day we were to close on the house and before I left I called Belinda and heard some despair in her voice. So, I asked what was wrong and she said she would tell me when I got home. When I got there, she couldn't hold it together any longer and showed me the papers showing the summary of closing, and the bottom line showed us owing money which was far different than the one we had before. I can still feel the breath leave my body in despair as tears whelped up in my eyes and hopelessness tried to show its face, but I wasn't going to allow that. Belinda was crying almost uncontrollably now, so I got on the phone to our realtor. She wasn't available to take the call but the person who answered got an earful. They were insistent that everything was correct. So, I told them we were going to back out of the sale which they said that we couldn't because all the paperwork was already signed.

We felt betrayed, misled, and was deeply hurt. We didn't have the money to cover what it stated we owed, and almost immediately I started praying and was rebuking the devil. He wasn't going to have us sell our house for a loss and be homeless with no money to get to Florida to start over again. We were dependent upon at least a few thousand dollars to hold us over for a short while and pay rent at the new place. But it all seemed gone now and we were devastated.

I was mad beyond mad now and the realtor finally called us and was playing it off like it was no big deal. I told her there was no way we could sell and that we were backing out, and she said by law we had to because the paperwork was in motion. She said she would work something out with a reassuring voice, but it did nothing for me. We were now broken and disgusted about the whole ordeal and considered not even showing up for the closing. But when we finally came to ourselves, we realized there was nothing we could do and just left it in God's hand.

As I reviewed the papers, we got that morning I noticed our realtor was getting a pretty big commission. Far greater than we discussed but we had nothing on paper recording it. About that time, she called and said she sent over another closing cost report. This time what we owed was much lower, but we still were shocked that we were going to have to pay anything at all. So, we humbly got ourselves pulled back together as best we could and headed to the title company to close on the house.

Belinda was hurt. I was furious. Yet somehow, we gave it to God and laid it at the altar believing that somehow He would work it out. We sat in the car outside the title company and prayed before going in. When we got inside, we talked to the realtor and she wasn't apologetic at all but said something about her employees needed to be paid. She had us backed up against a wall and we both knew it because we had nothing in writing about her commission (hard lesson learned for sure), but I stood my ground. I told her that we weren't signing anything and would just take whatever consequences that came along with that.

She looked shocked and was saying that we really didn't want to do that. Then said to give her a few minutes and left. When she came back there was new closing cost papers and this time it showed us getting around $1300 back instead of owing. She had changed her commission again and we knew it wouldn't get any better, so we accepted. We didn't like it for sure, but at least we could get out from under that house and live with our family again. The money would just get us to Florida and settle us in. The rest we placed in His care, trusting He would provide like He always had. He knew our heart's desires, and was making the way, just not quite as we had imagined it.

So, it was done. We sold our house in a dead market and defied all odds. What seemed impossible in the natural, was made possible by God's hand. I say hand because His hand, (His aligning of everything to work together for the good), was all over this. Even though the realtor, either intentionally or not, misled us and tried to take advantage of this sale, God still used it and factored it in with everything. It took me some time to find forgiveness for her, and I must admit there were times I hoped her business would fail. I wish I didn't have to go through those feelings, and I'm embarrassed over it. I repented of that too, but I know today that God allowed all of this to play out so we could move to Florida. I sometimes think this was her way of getting back at God for allowing her daughter to die by trying to deceive us. We know she was resentful and could see it in her, but to use God's children to somehow get back at Him wasn't the solution.

I pray she repented and turned back because we know she loved Him at one time.

Bittersweet seems to be a highly use word in transitioning, and I know I've used it in just about every move we've made. I guess because you are moving from something that will definitely be missed which is the bitter part, but it almost feels like you are being held down in some way. Like you have plateaued and there is no more growing yet knowing there is more out there, and freedom awaits. That's the sweet part. It really isn't a good word to use as I have had no regrets any place I have lived or left with a bad taste in my mouth, but I use the word because it describes being sad and happy at the same time.

We were excited to get back home in Florida and be with our family - to see where God would put us next - to follow a new path He had for us - to grow in ministry. At the same time, we were sad because we were leaving family in Kentucky and felt maybe we were "set for life" as far as our housing, jobs, and possessions were concerned. Going from stability to uncertainty is a huge walk of faith for sure, but for us it seemed to become the norm.

What should have been about a thirteen hour drive to Florida turned out to be closer to twenty-two. I was driving the moving truck full of our possessions pulling one car, and Belinda was driving the other with Buddy in it. Crossing over the Florida/Georgia line this time confirmed we were home, and what was just an impression in our spirits just a few weeks ago, was now a reality. Seeing the Winter Garden exit signs on the highway as we passed by them made me smile in anticipation with what God was planning. So finally, after a long delay because of a traffic accident, and only going on three hours of sleep, we made it into Orlando. Look at God! He did it! We were home!

The journey we went on in Kentucky lasted over five years and it turned full circle. We had no idea that we were only going on a temporary assignment. We just followed, and I was blessed and grateful I could be close to my Mom the last year of her life. Now we were back, and God restored much of what we sacrificed when we first went into the ministry. Our cars - our furniture - guitars and music equipment - and now our family.

God doesn't always, or should I say He rarely, shows us the end from the beginning. He gives us stages, or phases to act upon and we can't skip any along the way. We must stay on the path He has for us regardless how it contradicts the world around us. Our time in Kentucky was for a season and it was a steppingstone onto something else, even though we thought it was permanent.

Confusion was probably with a lot of people with opening and closing the church - with helping the other church and then pulling out - buying a brand new house and then selling it three and a half years later - leaving great jobs to move and face new job searches. To the world it probably looked like we were stuck in indecisiveness, but to us we were following God's leading and there was nothing haphazard in our thinking at all. Eleven years had passed from the time God spoke to us to close our businesses and sell out to that time we pulled back into Florida.

So much had transpired in a short time, and we probably wrote more chapters in our lives then than some have in a lifetime.

We have heard the saying to "exercise our faith", and did we ever. It seemed like when we started to feel settled and comfortable in a place, God had our faith go in a different direction. We all know exercise can be painful, but it is beneficial. Right? Without exercising we can deteriorate and become weak. The Bible says we all have a measure of faith (Ref. Rom. 12:3), and that measure needs to grow. It won't get big all on its own, but it has to be stretched to the point where it hurts. Where it may be sore for a short time. To where it feels that we have exerted all we have. But after a time of recouping, we find out that we are stronger. That we can go further than before. What used to make us get sore and hurt, doesn't affect us much anymore.

So, for us to pick up and move again didn't seem out of reach. We had seen God move before and provide, and now our faith level was stronger than when we first started our walk with Him. Sure, we felt our spiritual muscles hurting some, but even though the load that we were carrying was heavier than before, we could carry it now. That little voice of doubt that maybe God wouldn't step in like He had done before, was getting more faint to hear. Instead of "hoping" God would provide we waited with anticipation "how" He was going to provide.

We got settled into our new place knowing God did it. He sold our house and He got us there. We didn't have the money we thought we were going to have, but that didn't limit Him. Man wasn't our source. He was. The job I had in Kentucky at my brother's business was a blessing for sure, and every year-end he would give me a bonus. When we left Kentucky the end of the year was five months away and I sure wasn't expecting anything, but I believe God spoke to him. He sent me a check with the bonus I would have gotten if I stayed there, and it was very humbling. We had many other miracles in our finances which were hugs from God and the assurance that He had this. Unexpected checks came from our home insurance premium, car insurance, and we even got a check for a utility deposit from when we lived in Florida six years prior that we had no idea about. It was getting exciting to go to the mailbox.

Belinda was having a hard time getting a job and it seemed every turn was a dead end for her. She had felt a witness about a job for the same company she worked at in Kentucky, only to find out that her previous boss marked her as not re-hirable. It wasn't done intentionally, but the way the questionnaire was worded for exiting employees, there was no space to mention that she had been out on medical leave. But then she remembered a letter she received from the HR department stating that she was indeed re-hirable, and after some digging for it through emails, we found it. So, she presented it to the store manager, and she got the job starting as an assistant. God did it again even though the enemy tried to stop it. He gave Belinda favor and guess where the store was located? Yes, in Winter Garden.

I was able to start working out of the apartment for my brother's business. That was a miracle in itself, as I thought my camera repair days were over, but then he approached me and asked if I would consider helping him from Florida. He would send me work and even though it was only part time, God made our money stretch, and never once did we neglect to pay our tithe even for the smallest of blessings.

Apartment life was an adjustment for sure, but knowing that the noisy neighbors that lived above us was family was OK by me. We were no longer separated from them and God was working it out for us to get settled again. The past faith walk had its highs and lows for sure, and through what seemed like a chaotic journey, God was in control. If He could do it in times past, He could do it again. Belinda not only got a job back with the same company, but it was a full time position with benefits. We both agreed that I should just keep on working out of the apartment for my brother instead of seeking employment somewhere else for the time being. God supplied all our needs and as we stepped out in faith to move back to Florida, God honored it. We were home, and it felt fantastic!

Chapter 9
Replanted

As we were searching for a new church home, I was reminded of what the Lord spoke to me the first morning in our new place during my devotion time. He spoke two words deep into my spirit - "Study. Pray". He spoke it strong and with clarity. Almost like a branding iron, searing it in. I was doing it already, but I heard it several times, so I knew in this new season, this was to be my main focus.

The next day in my daily Bible reading, I read in Jeremiah, *"But I will gather the remnant of My flock out of all countries where I have driven them, and bring them back to their folds; and they shall be fruitful and increase. I will set up shepherds over them who will feed them; and they shall fear no more, nor be dismayed, nor shall they be lacking," says the LORD."* Jer. 23:3-4. It spoke directly into my spirit like God placed those verses there just for me. So I wrote down in my Bible notes, "God spoke this to me the day after we moved back to Orlando, July of 2011, that He brought us back to our fold to go further in ministry, and that we were going to have teachers over us, and we would not fear or be in lack."

I know these verses were in context to the dispersion of the nation of Israel by shepherds (Godly leaders) that scattered God's flock, but God very vividly revealed to me something else. This is what He spoke to me in a little more detail to what I wrote in my notes; "I have gathered you from Kentucky where I have lead you to for My purpose, and brought you back to your folds (place/home in Florida), and you shall be fruitful and prosper. I will setup shepherds over you who will feed you spiritual things, and you will fear no more and be confident that I will provide for you. You will no longer feel shattered or downcast, and you shall no longer live in the land of lack both spiritually and financially".

Some may think that's a stretch to interpret God's Word like that, but I have received revelation from His Word while reading it many times. I mean, I still know the context, and in no way intend to change the meaning or teach contrary to it, but He does speak to us in unique ways sometimes while reading it. That's one of the reasons it's called the "living word". I was deeply touched that day (which is just a different way of saying I wept), and a sense of peace as only He can give, filled my inner most being. It was a strong confirmation that we were in His plans to move back to Florida.

For our dog Buddy, it was quite the change for him with being the only dog now, but also there was no backyard to run and play in. So, every time he had to go out, it involved putting him on a leash and walking him. The blessing behind it all was even though we were living in Orlando, there was a college next to us where I could take him into a big field area with lots of open space, and huge oak trees too. I called it my oasis in the big city, but it was actually my new prayer closet.

Having to take him out many times during the day was exercise for my body, but it was also exercise for my spiritual being. I would just walk for acres and acres, praying and praising God.

Having a job that I could work from home was a tremendous blessing too. I could care for him during his grieving, and get him acclimated to the new living arrangements; but mostly it also gave me the ability to do what God spoke to me - study and pray. He gave me the time to do it now and I was determined not to waste the opportunity. Our jobs were sustaining us, and we were still going week to week on our bills, yet God was faithful to provide.

We visited a few churches, and nothing really surfaced that "this was the one", until we broadened our search to guess where? Yes! Winter Garden. This was an exceptionally friendly church and the pastor there preached powerful, relevant messages. I could tell he didn't just open a book of sermons, closed his eyes and pointed, but sought God on what to preach. We were able to share our ministry experiences with him some, and over lunch one day he asked me to preach that Sunday night. I was taken away by the invite and broke down before God later that day out walking in my new prayer closet. He had a plan for us again.

I was amazed that the same way I was asked to preach in Kentucky, I was asked again there. It was starting to not look coincidental but purposed by Him. I never solicited myself to preach, but God spoke to these pastors to ask me to take the mic for a service and beyond, and entrusted me to their people. I was more than humbled. I had a deep down aching in my spirit that was crying, "are You sure You have the right person Lord?" But once I started moving as His minister, He confirmed that He knew what He was doing by the way the people were blessed, and I take no credit in that at all. It was all Him through me, and He gets all the praise and glory for it.

So, I started helping the pastor with the audio equipment, recorded the services, and reproduced them on CD's. We were still personally struggling financially, and the extra gas to Winter Garden was a concern. He gave us a few dollars every now and then and even though we declined, he insisted that we take it. So, it seemed every time we were a little short he would bless us, and there were even some church members that would give us a Pentecostal handshake. We weren't beggars or even hinted that we needed help, but God would speak to them and would use them to supplement our finances. It was humbling for sure and it felt weird to take money from them, but we knew it was God behind it and part of His provisions for us. We were reaping some of the seeds we had sown along the way.

We were there for a few months and one night after the service I waited for the pastor to give him back his laptop, which we used to record the services, and he seemed very distant. He only spoke for a minute and wasn't his normal peppy self. I asked if he was okay and it looked like he was wanting to share something, but then asked me if I ever had any experience dealing with church board members and left it at that. I didn't know what he meant but later found out that either the church had let him go, or that he resigned. I didn't ask for details or pressed to know why, all they told me was that he decided to move back to Tennessee.

I was shocked by the whole ordeal and was saddened, because I really liked him and felt this could have been a landing pad for a while. There was really no one else in the church that could fill his shoes. They had a lot of board members but no ministers. They came to me and asked if I would be interested in preaching and teaching on Wednesday nights, as well as leading that night's song service, and also helping with the praise team for the other services. They had another minister they were bringing in from the outside to preach on Sunday's and asked if I could open and close those services and take up the offerings too. I was more than excited and remembered my vow I made to the Lord, that I would never turn down an opportunity to preach.

So, I enthusiastically said yes and was taken back even more when they said there was a small salary involved as well. Just like my usual self, I was ready to blurt out that they didn't need to, and the Holy Spirit restrained my tongue. He impressed in me that this was His plan, and I felt this was the main reason God told me to study and pray. Through all that time, God supplemented our income, and I knew it wasn't by chance I was at the right place at the right time, but in His perfect will.

Everything felt great and there I was - in God's plan – in Florida - in Winter Garden. I had been through the heartache of closing our church in Kentucky. Been through the heartache of being used by the other church. Been through the lonely times of not being involved in a church. Fought through the darkest time in my life and now here I was not only helping this church, but helping to lead it by His grace. For the first time in my ministerial life I was being paid a salary to preach, and the gap in our finances was filled once again.

Now I can't remember if it was when the board first asked me to help, but I heard during that time the Spirit say, "hireling". It was confusing to me at first, but after I pondered on it, I knew that God only had me there for a season, as they were in the process of looking for another lead pastor. I did what I could to help whole-heartedly. Every service I would open - help in the music or lead worship - take up the offering - preach on Wednesday nights - and then close the services. I also attended music practice and planning meetings. Every week I would change the marquee sign with an encouraging message. I was an integral part of the church as I also made hospital visits. It felt like we had landed, and I soon forgot, or maybe I pretended I never heard that word "hireling". Regardless, God was using me, and it felt great.

With this new assignment that God intricately put together, I had to study and pray almost constantly. My prayer walks with Buddy in the field and through the neighborhood became more and more impassioned. I felt the burden of the people at that church, and my burden for souls and their spiritual growth would consume me at times. I was now in a position to make a difference and was full-steam to do so. Going on those walks with the nightly Florida sunsets was almost majestic, and was probably one of the most intense seasons of my prayer life thus far.

There was a certain area in the neighborhood that I used to cut through, and with Buddy after sunset, his guard would kick into level ten. So, I would have to avoid running into people and would walk off of the main areas. Florida is full of retention ponds to help with the rain drainage, and in this area, there were two of them side by side with only a thin path between. When walking through I would get consumed with God's presence, and at times, I would just weep and pray. The skyline showed the stars so beautifully, which is rare in a big city, and I could never just pass through. I would have to stop and pray to the God that created what I saw before me. This was a spot on my walk I could really touch Jesus and feel His compassion for souls - for the church people - for my family - the lost... I agonized in prayer and pleaded and worshipped Him there.

I never shared that spot with anybody, or even talked about it, not even with Belinda then. That was where I poured myself out to God, and where God would pour into me. I cried so much and agonized there that I called the place, "the weeping ponds". Sometimes I would pace back and forth - sometimes I would sit – other times kneel with my hands raised up to Him... Buddy must have thought I was crazy as all he wanted to do was walk, but I think after a short time of doing that, he started to expect the stop. God gave me messages to preach and a more intimate prayer experience there. Sometimes, I just prayed in my heavenly language and bore the heaviness of others as I interceded.

For seven months that was my church, so much that the delay in finding a pastor seemed more distant. So, I applied for the position and turned in my résumé thinking maybe they were waiting for me to do so. I thought it strange that I never got a response back, and then the members on the board almost started to avoid me. Now the other minister that preached on Sundays was never involved with anything else, not because he didn't want to, but because he was up in age and didn't live close by. He just came and preached and put his time in until they could find someone. He even asked me one time why I didn't take the position. When I told him I applied for it but never got a response, he looked more disheartened than I did. He knew my heart and my passion for the people there.

Then I heard from one of the church members in a casual conversation that they were bringing a preacher in for the position. Even they looked surprised that I didn't know about it. As you can imagine, I was hurt, and it cut me to the bone. It hurt so bad that after my usual Wednesday night I expressed to a few board members how I felt about them ignoring my application. How I felt betrayed without any explanation from them why they dismissed me. How I did not appreciate them being honest with me that they had a pastor on the way.

I had put so much into that church with hopes that maybe I could be their pastor. They never did give me a reason for their silence through it all, so that same night I packed up all my stuff and told them I wasn't coming back. They knew I wasn't happy, and it almost didn't phase them. They were so cold and in the back of my mind I could faintly hear the word, "hireling". It didn't ease the pain immediately, but God did warn me at the beginning of it all that I was there on a temporary assignment. Maybe I should have never gotten so hopeful, and I probably should have just stayed there to support their decision, but I couldn't get over feeling betrayed and used. It hurt, and it hurt bad.

Now a "hireling" is simply someone that is paid to do a job. A hired laborer. I know I heard that in my spirit seven months earlier when they asked me to help, but it never occurred to me that was all they wanted me for. I felt maybe I was no different than the lawn service people. I poured myself out and never thought of my service to them as employment, but as unto the Lord shepherding His people.

The check I received every week wasn't from a job, but a direct blessing from God to sustain our finances. I would have helped them without any payment as I had done in Kentucky with that other church. Ministry has never been about income for me, but about the outcome. So even though things didn't turn out, it was still God's plan. Those dear saints needed my help and I was available. Not all of them were cold and I cherish the time I was there, and have since forgiven those I was offended by, and counted it all joy to have served them.

My decision to leave that church in Winter Garden impacted our income, but after praying through everything that transpired, I knew I had to pull out so that the new pastor could easily fall into his role as leader. If I would have stayed, I probably would have been a hindrance because of the feelings I harbored. So, because I knew it was in God's plan to leave, I knew He would provide and he did, as Belinda started to make bonuses at her job. Our income was supplemented by that, along with God's grace and favor. His provision came into perfect alignment again for us.

Once more, I was overcome with feelings of loneliness, but still pressed through. I was starting to really learn that God just doesn't have one plan for us, but His word says that He knows the "plans" He has for us. (Ref. Jer. 29:11AMP). Yes. "Plans". Plural. Like in many. A lot. Like the word "plan" but with an "s" on the end of it. He knows that we may travel on many paths in life - and that maybe we will drift off course and be lured into a different direction - that maybe we will give up a plan because our flesh is weak - that maybe we will stay at one place too long when we were supposed to move on... but there is another plan waiting for us.

He knows ahead of time about all our plans and the ones we'd mess up. Nothing takes Him by surprise, and he just doesn't have a couple of backup plans, but as many as it takes for us to continue in Him. He may also have plans for us which requires completely starting over again. A different career or relocating to a different city or church. An end of one season and the start of another. We don't mess up those plans, but He steps in and changes things around. He might allow that we will be rejected which forces us to leave a plan. Not something we may have botched, but a season and a trial setup by Him to shape us into His ultimate purpose. A plan that modes us on His potter's wheel. What might look like a failure, is really a process He has designed to shape us for the next plan, and there has to be a completion of one plan so the next one can start.

Our lease where we were staying at was coming to an end and we started searching for a new home. We were praying for one with a backyard because even though I didn't mind too much walking Buddy several times a day, physically it was taxing on my body. We did find a place which was bigger than where we were staying with a backyard, and it was really close to Belinda's work. Yes, it was in Winter Garden too. God worked it out again as the price wasn't a whole lot more than what we were already paying.

During this time, I prayed and fasted a lot seeking God's next plan. It's been said that when God closes one door that He opens another one, but the hardest part I believe is being in the hallway. The feelings of waiting and the seclusion of no doors being opened at all, is both lonely and exciting. My biggest hurdle was learning this. I used to get in the hallway and just weep and cry in my pity party not even looking up to see if maybe there was a light on through a door, or even knowing there were other doors for that matter. My hallway experiences weren't getting any easier, but I went from thinking once the door was shut behind me that was it, to seeing a hallway full of doors and possibilities. Then waiting for one to open revealing the next plan.

When a door closes there is that thinking of, "what did I do to deserve this? - Everything was going so good - NOW WHAT?!?!". Closed doors are possibilities to enter new doors, and we can't enter into a new door without exiting the previous one. Whether we exit them on our own accord or were forced out of them, we can't change the fact that the door is closed. Trying to barge back in and reclaim what we had will only lead to despair because we will be out of God's will. That season has been closed unless we made a mistake and have to go back.

Sitting in the hallway is the beginning of God showing us the next door, and in that, sitting patiently. Not with our arms crossed demanding an instant answer but waiting for God to perfectly align the new plan. I know we live in an instant society with same day delivery, but special orders take time. They aren't massed produced so extra preparation and attention is needed before they can be processed for delivery. So, while we wait, we can prepare ourselves by seeking the Maker of plans and by knowing Him more.

Patience also is not something we inherently have; it's produced by the testing of our faith as James stated in his Epistle. (Ref. James 1:3). You see, waiting for God to direct us is a process. A runner trains by running. As Christians, we hear God by listening. By training ourselves to wait for His promptings. To have an ear out. Every dog we have had sleeps with one ear open. They look like they are resting, but then they hear something that makes them jump up and they act upon it. Waiting in anticipation to hear something. So, must we with God. Patiently waiting for direction by constantly listening.

During this time of waiting on the Lord I felt myself starting to fall back into depression. Working out of the apartment and Belinda being gone lots played a toll on me for sure. With being by myself for a good part of the time and not serving anywhere was miserable to say the least. The devil played mind games with me even though I constantly rebuked them, but I felt I missed the mark in ministry again. Like maybe I had done something wrong, but I knew I was in God's will every single time. Still, I questioned God and was deeply hurt again, going through the cycles of various thoughts. Wondering why it was just another touch-and-go landing. Wondering if I would ever be used again in ministry. Wondering what my next steps were going to be and lead me to.

I had often toiled with the idea of going back to the church we had just left a few months ago. The people there were great, but I still had a few hurts stirring within me from the way it ended.

Belinda would casually mention that maybe we should go back and visit, just to socialize with believers, and that it would do us good. The seclusion was really eating me up inside and she could see it even though I tried to hide it. So, I remember crying out to God in prayer telling Him how lonely I was - how I hated being idle and not using my talents for the Kingdom - then, yelling through the pain and tears I told him, "I don't want to keep going through this!" He then so clearly spoke into my spirit, calmly, yet commanding these words, "then don't!"

I'm not sure if even God got tired of being at my pity party and rebuked me, or if it was a word of release, but it shook me up out of my despair and made sense. For me to break free from all I was going through, I had to do something. Yes, me. I was waiting on God, but He was waiting on me to get to the point of being so fed up that I, (yes, me again), would have to initiate the next move. I believe it was His plan to go back to that church, and He knew I wasn't going to go back until I was broken. Broken of the hurts and ill feelings I had. He had to wait for me to get stripped all the way down to me needing them, instead of them needing me. I needed a time-out in the hallway and had to go back into the door I exited. This next plan was going to be a U-turn.

So, very apprehensively on a Wednesday night we went back, not knowing if they would receive us or not. It was so humbling because I knew I was admitting I was wrong. It took a lot of courage to go back and walk through those doors, but we did, and they received us with loving arms. The new pastor greeted us, and it seemed like we were supposed to be there again. It was different being sort of a bystander but that didn't last long. Before I knew it, I was back on the praise team switching between drums on Sunday morning, and playing guitar on Wednesday and Sunday nights. I never asked them if I could help but they asked me, so I knew it was God.

The pastor and his wife were young, and they really loved the Lord and fit right in. He played keyboards and led the praise team but after a while, he trusted me to lead them on Sunday nights. It felt really good to be back, he even had me preach a couple of times, but there was a part of me that knew it was temporary again. During this time, even though I was helping and part of the church, we never really felt like we were all the way in. Like it was another touch-and-go. It got awkward at times around the pastor and a few board members. I'm not really sure of the reasons, but it was definitely different than the first time we were there. Like almost a coldness or maybe they just had their guard up, and we felt all alone even though we served side by side with them. Like we were outsiders in a way.

I was feeling that we were being stifled and held down, and that God had so much more for us. The church wasn't growing, nor did they really have a solid plan for growing yet. I had a passion inside that was like the prophet Jeremiah spoke of: …"*But His word was in my heart like a burning fire shut up in my bones; I was weary of holding it back, And I could not*". Jeremiah 20:9. Deep down inside I knew I needed to go forward and was feeling to start our own ministry. We did it before in Kentucky, and it just seemed right to try again in Winter Garden.

Every New Year's I commit to a three day fast. I like to start on New Year's Eve praising God and reflecting on the year we were coming out of and go into the new year seeking Him for guidance. This time I really purposed for His will and plan as I was feeling torn on which direction to go in, and I didn't want to make a wrong decision. One of the entry's I wrote in my journal was:

> "Lord, help me to be open to whatever You speak to me. Take away all fear. Remind me of what's at the finish line. I reject all doubt, apprehension, and walls. I'm tired of not having peace in ministry. Give me <u>clear</u>, unwavering direction… I pour my heart out to Your counsel. Clean me up. Take out garbage. Put in precious gems… Open my thoughts and mind, and don't let flesh be an influence".

There were a few other things I was praying for but the main one was if I was to stay there. It almost tormented me and because there was not much peace, I needed to sort out if it was me, or something else causing my double-mindedness. I didn't get a lot of definite answers on that fast, but I was able to confirm that God was wanting us to move on, but not just yet. So, we were waiting for a release and also during that fast, I was feeling in my spirit to start a Bible study. Belinda had mentioned that community clubhouses were an option. I even spoke to someone at the District they said that was how they started their church. It branched from weekly meetings at their clubhouse in their apartment complex. So, we met with the manager where we lived and shared what we were wanting to do, and they said they would present it before the board, and they approved it. Around four AM one morning, God woke me up and gave me the name "Christian Unity Center" for the Bible study.

I still stayed helping the other church, but I felt the separation starting to take place, and I was reading a lot about starting ministries. So, as I prayed about what kind of ministry we were to have, God gave me more details about it. But He was mostly dealing with me and doing it in my brokenness and hurt. He started showing me what not to be more than what to be. "I need faith so strong; emotions don't move it!" is what I wrote in my journal during that time. Peter's faith got him on the water, and he started walking on it, but his emotions (his mind and thoughts) made him sink. I knew I had to move on, but I was starting to get comfortable there again. My mind and thoughts held me back until I decided it was time to get back on the water and trust Him.

Immediately I went into another three day fast and battled physically and spiritually with great fierceness from the enemy, as he was not letting up. My journal entry read:

> "I cried really hard tonight. I hope He speaks to me in the night or morning. I can't take this much more. I'm broken so much it hurts deep inside, a painful anguish. I just want to know what I'm supposed to do in life... I feel the timing of it all is slipping away. I don't know what else I can do. He has to speak to me clearly and strongly".

I ended the fast about eight hours early and heard a pastor on TV preaching about the potter and the clay in Jeremiah 18 and it pierced my soul. I realized that God was reforming me like clay on the wheel. He assured me that He was in control and was fixing to fill this empty vessel. Now the vessel has to go through the fire and there is no other way to complete it, and I felt that's what I was going through. The fire.

A few days later there was a guest evangelist at the church and preached a message about God not being done with us yet.

It spoke straight into me and God held true to His word that says, He is "the lifter up of my head". (Ref. Psalms 3:3 KJV). God had encouraged me through two different preachers and gave me timely words. I'm not sure I can count the many times I heard the right message at the right time, and felt God speaking directly to me through it.

So, after I had gotten back up from being down and had a renewed sense of purpose, even though I had no idea what direction God was going to steer me in, I felt strengthened to do anything. If he wanted me to stay at the church and help, I would. If He wanted us to start a new work through a Bible Study gathering at our townhome clubhouse, I would. I just needed to gently get off the see-saw of decisions and move on, without doubt trying to knock me off.

The pastor asked me out to lunch, and I was hoping to hammer things out as to where or if I fit in there, as I felt the Bible study was taking more of a backseat then. I shared with him openly, being transparent as I could, about my desire for outreach and possibly moving on. He then asked if I would be interested in becoming their Director of Evangelism and we both looked at each other and felt this could be both our prayers answered. I held back the excitement inside because I didn't want to jump right in and say yes until I really sought God on it, so I told him I would pray about it.

During that time, I was also involved with the District and the Bishop called and asked if I wanted to become presbyter over the central Florida area. They had a few churches I would oversee, and I immediately felt overwhelmed and told him too I had to pray about it. These offerings of ministry work that came back to back just made things really complicated. I was grateful for sure but was fearful of making a wrong decision.

We were paying our tithe to the district, and to come on board at the church meant we'd have to pay it there. So, I would have to leave the district if I took the church position. But if I left the district, I wouldn't have their backing if we started a new work. I was pulled in a lot of directions, so it was back to intense prayer. I had many decisions. I went from not having any ministry opportunities, to multiple ones. I prayed hard and sought God over it all, weighed out all the pros and cons, then finally I felt God telling me that I needed to choose. Yes, me.

Sometimes in our walks of faith, God gives us several paths we can go down, and He lets us make the decision. As easy as it would be to just follow His lead and let Him decide, other times He leaves it to us. I guess He'd rather us put our heart and soul into something we want, than possibly, grudgingly take the path that we may feel He forced us into. Just like when I had to decide to close my business or not. I actually took the harder road, and this is what I felt I needed to do this time as well.

It would have been so easy to take the position at the church but as I was praying, I started to feel like we would be stifled if we stayed. That maybe we would be settling. Yes, we could finally land, but it wouldn't be the right pad. So, I told the pastor there that the only way it could happen would be if Belinda would be by my side helping - that they would compensate me in some way (I wasn't looking for a salary. Just an occasional love offering). I also required keeping my position with the District and keep our tithes going there as I was also considering the presbyter position. During our meeting things got tense at times and he told me that we needed to be members there by their rules meaning our tithes to. He basically was going to direct everything and more or less just wanted a volunteer. I won't share all the details, but I felt the door wasn't shutting, it was being slammed.

They sure were expecting a lot from me and I felt I had poured myself out already. But for me to give up my ministerial papers to assume a new title was asking even more. An ultimatum is what was presented before me and that's pretty much what I had given them. So, there was no middle ground where I could keep my papers and become a member of that church. As much as I would have loved to have been "Director of Evangelism", it would have been by title only.

In part of processing all that was going on, this is what I wrote in my journal. Now, I'm not sharing this to invite people to a pity party, but because walks of faith involve getting blisters on our feet, and getting rid of the old shoes before we can slide the new ones on:

> "I guess the door is shut at the church. Time to move on and get off of Easy Road and get on Road of Faith. Feeling crushed. I really wanted this road, but I guess God has faith for me with bigger, harder tasks. So tired of being hurt and used by people. At least I got more ministerial experience, and really, I was working for the Kingdom. I thought knowing what to do next would give some peace. I guess I need some time to heal first".

So that was it. The decision to leave and pursue the Bible study became a reality. I also took the presbyter position with the District and it all felt right, even though it was definitely the harder road to be on. As we were preparing for this new work, things were falling into place with clear direction from God. Probably clearer than it had ever been before. One of the other pastors in the District said he wanted to help with costs on the clubhouse rental which humbled me so much because we didn't have much startup money. So that was a huge, huge blessing. Flyers were printed, the website went up, a FaceBook page was created, and planning was going great except we didn't get the day we wanted to hold the Bible study, so we had to take Friday nights. That raised a concern, but we went for it anyways.

There were approximately 300 townhomes in the community we lived at, and without help from anybody, because Belinda was working, I knocked on about half of them one Saturday morning. I must tell you that took some courage to do, as I am not that kind of person. That was way outside of my comfort zone. As much as I tried to tell God I didn't want to, especially to go alone, He gave me the strength. It was very awkward at first, but after I got over the nervousness it went very well. I got a few cold shoulders, but I also got some positive responses. The following Saturday we both went out and did some old-fashioned door knocking, which you just don't see anymore. But it's what God told me to do. Jesus told His disciples in the book of Acts to "go", so that's what we did.

I would walk the neighborhood with Buddy and pray, pray, and pray for God to move in that community. I mean I felt it strong to start this work. I knew I had to give it my all, as this was an opportune time in our lives, as I wasn't working but a few hours a week out of the house and made really good money doing it. Something inside of me said this could be my last attempt, that this could be the last chance in my life to do this, so I had to get it right and get it going.

All I wanted was to serve God in the capacity He trained me in. Some people go to colleges to get their doctorate degrees, but I never had that. God schooled me in real time, in real ministry. This was Him doing it through me not some idea I had or a profession I thought I'd ever choose. In a book I read about spiritual leadership, it was said that spiritual leaders serve because they are drawn by God's Spirit, not because they fancy themselves there, or a sense of compulsion, or a sense of being driven. In God's timing they are brought into the leadership He has chosen for them.

So, I was on fire once again for the Kingdom and had great faith that He was doing it. The call on our lives was getting ready to start over in a new capacity in Winter Garden. Through much prayer and fasting's, I sensed that a solid plan was coming to fruition. I felt so strong about it that I sold my custom made electric guitar to help fund the Bible study that I believed was going to eventually turn into a church. It had taken about two months to get everything lined up and we were ready for our first service.

Friday night came and we went down to the clubhouse to get ready. We setup tables, chairs, and even brought some snacks and refreshments. I brought my acoustic guitar, as I planned to sing a few songs for praise and worship, teach with prepared material including handouts, and then close by inviting souls to come to Jesus and pray for those wanting prayer. We waited and nobody was there at the starting time, so we just did what we did in Kentucky at our church there and started anyways like we had a full house.

Belinda opened in prayer and I went through the short song service and still, nobody was there. We let about twenty minutes go by and could tell it was just going to be us three; Belinda, myself, and Jesus. It was kind of discouraging, actually, it knocked the wind out of me for a few days, but we had faith for the next service. The next morning, I had to dust myself off and preach at a prayer breakfast, and then preach again Sunday at one of the churches I oversaw which might have been the strongest I ever preached, with five people giving their lives to Jesus. Only God got me through, and He certainly did it.

Then at our second Bible study, nobody showed up again. This time it hurt pretty bad as we had put so much effort into it and felt this was His will and plan. Maybe it was the scheduled day and time? If we had Sundays, maybe it would have been a different outcome. I'm not really sure? To say I was discouraged and heartbroken would be a gross understatement. We had poured so much into this with my time and our finances. It was back to the land of "now what?". I thought this was it. This is where all the roads were leading us to, but it was now seeming to be a dead end.

I know this is supposed to be a book on faith, but I'm going to get really real here. If anyone ever thought walks of faith would be easy, they soon learn that they are the most emotionally challenging experiences they can go through. *"I can do all things through Christ who strengthens me"* (Phil. 4:13), doesn't become just a simple motto or creed, it becomes our life's blood and the bone marrow that holds us together when we feel unworthy, underequipped, and underqualified. It becomes who we are.

My next journal entry:

"Don't know what to do? So tired of the disappointment. Don't know where I missed God. I feel more embarrassed than anything. Tired of the start-and-goes that don't last. I really need a breakthrough, direction, help, or something. All I want is to use these God-given talents to help others, worship Him, and see souls saved. Why does it have to be so hard? When will I land? Just when I climb out of one heartbreak, the next one seems worse. I don't know what I missed or where I'm lacking? Too many eyes are upon me to prove God is real through this. What would it profit to fail, but that others would think God is not real? I KNOW You're real God! I'm not doing all of this for anything but because You called me too. Sorry if I may say something that offends You, but I'm so tired of being in the valley, the desert, the wilderness… Holy Spirit help me to have better understanding and guidance". (Then a few days later I wrote): "God is going to have to beat me up pretty bad with His voice if He wants me to continue in faith with this. I keep saying, "I'm over it! I'm over it!" I don't want to be, especially with so many eyes on us. I want people to see God move in this so they can see the God I serve. So tired of hurting trying to serve in ministry. It's my heart's desire. I just want to go home to Jesus if He's done with me. Help me Jesus!"

I told you I was going to get really real. That's what I was feeling at the time in my journal writing. So, after a few more Friday nights, we closed it down. Not one person showed up for any of the services. Seemed all the hard work, finances, and sacrifices we had made just left us alone and beaten, and I was not about to go through another ministry experience like that again any time soon. So, in my despair I told God, "I'm over it!" Not over Him, but over the touch-and-go landings. My frustrated outcry left me repenting that I got mad at Him. Yes, I meant it when I said it multiple times, but deep in my spirit I didn't want to be over it, but into it.

There we were again with no church home and nowhere to serve. I got in so deep and gave it my all for these faith walks and was left thinking: maybe we could have kept the church open in Kentucky a little longer and pushed harder - maybe we could have looked beyond the other church's doctrine and stayed longer - maybe I could have eaten humble pie and supported the board's decision in choosing a pastor? Maybe I could have left the district to help that church with leading their outreach? Maybe we could have tried the Bible study one more service?

The pressures of everything was barreling down on me and our finances was hurting bad. So bad it was causing strife in our marriage. Almost as quick as my soul was cast down, I tried to get back up. Much quicker than in times past, but it was still a process of healing, and it didn't hurt any less. After the dust settled in my emotions, I was feeling, (actually, it was more of a revelation) that the Bible study was a test from God. A test of faith, but I wasn't quite sure why.

Sort of like Abraham and Isaac. Abraham must have thought, "God, why did You have me travel for three days and raise my knife to my son, and have me go through all the trauma of it all just to provide an escape that you planned all along?" But Abraham had to go for two reasons; so, God could see how faithful he was, and so Abraham could see how faithful God was. Tests aren't just for the one giving the test, but also for the one taking it. So, both can see how much has been learned and experienced.

God knew from the very beginning of the Bible study inception that it was but a test for me. So much planning, prep work, and sacrifice went forth, but at the very end, God was testing my faith. He was sharpening and developing my faith skills. This time He was training us, much like in a drill or in a military field exercise. We went full scale into following His directions, and for whatever reason He hasn't revealed yet, we went through the motions of starting a church again. I may not ever get insight why the test, but I did learn through it all what was needed to better hear Him when He calls which is: fasting, prayer, listening, and total trust in Him.

I'm not sure what the world was thinking the many times we started into something but then it ended. Hopefully, they saw our faith and love for Jesus, and our desire to serve Him regardless of where the journey went. I know I felt a release in my spirit from these assignments and wished they were my landing pad, but back up off the ground we went time after time. The desire to land was even more consuming to me, as we had met a lot of saints along the way but didn't have many true friends. Really, we had no one to confide in and share our experiences that we thought would understand. Our ventures were far different than the norm of ministry work.

I remember praying, and praying, and praying for God to line up something for us. Seemed we could never connect with the right people that walked the same roads we had. Everyone was grounded, and had been grounded, but we were always the people that didn't stay long. Not because we didn't want to either. The ground we trod seemed so vastly different, and I don't think everyone got us. I really don't think anyone got us.

We were, and are called to be, helps. Drifters in a way. Nomads for His Kingdom maybe? "People without fixed habitation" as defined, and that's what we felt like. I always refer back to touch-and-go landings because that is the best way to describe our ministerial life. My heart yearned to land - my soul cried to land - my spirit agonized to land because I got tired of questioning God, but then He always confirmed that we were called to these places for seasons. I remember crying out to Him many times asking, "why can't we just land?", and never got a response.

Right after this, now I was not looking for another job at that time, but Belinda's store manager came to us and asked if I would be interested in an overnight stocking job at one of the other stores. I knew him from Belinda working there and he knew I had experience. So, I accepted and planned on it only being for a short time just to supplement our income until I could figure out my next life's plan. I was still working at my brother's business from the home, but that was slowing down, and I was still overseeing a couple of churches in the district too. Life was busy, probably a little too busy, but I still had this void inside that I needed to fill.

Chapter 10
The Landing

During this time in the hallway again, I made my prayers pointed, specifically for a church home that we could land, and to meet a couple our age to serve with. To become friends with them and not just be someone to be called on only when something was needed. I felt our lives were getting to a point that if we didn't land soon, our window of opportunities would run out. I found myself alone lots again and felt a dire need to serve in ministry even more than before. After all, here I was, a presbyter and no church home. The churches I oversaw were too far away to attend regularly and I really needed a home base for many reasons.

The new job I had stocking was an adjustment with working overnights, and the thought of doing that job as a career for the rest of my life and not being in ministry concerned me lots. We had just made a push to start a new work with the Bible study, and even though we seized the moment, I felt another favorable opportunity may not recur, as getting older, needing to consider our later years, and our financial security was getting to be more in the foreground.

So back to square one again, and the daunting task to find a home church continued. We visited a few places, but nothing seemed to be the "right" one. So out of desperation again, I turned to the advertisements for churches needing musicians like I did in Kentucky, thinking maybe we could find a church that needed help. Somewhere I could use my talents He blessed me with for His Kingdom. I got almost an immediate response from a church needing musicians, so I reached back out to them with lots of questions and we met. I wasn't going to go through another time of wondering what a church believed, so I was up front and very direct with my questions on their beliefs, and they were right in-line with ours.

So, a reach of desperation turned out to be God's hand directing us. We were all around the same age, and the pastor and his wife just recently closed their church in a nearby city to start a new one, and guess where? Yes. Winter Garden. We visited with them and at the time they were holding services in their living room. From that day forward, we believed that was where God wanted us to be, and we soon found out they were launching out and was going to share a space with another church. I was starting to think this was my answered prayer about meeting a couple our age that we could serve with.

Weeks turned into months, and before long we felt we needed to make it official and join the church. I didn't feel right about having to pay our tithes to the district office we were a part of, I always felt tithes needed to stay in the same zip code and that's what I told the pastor. He mentioned that they could get us ministerial papers and with that, I felt a strong leading of the Lord to resign from the District and my presbyter position, so we officially came on board.

Belinda was ordained as a minister and I was ordained as an elder. I was even asked to join the church board too. What seemed like an extremely hard decision to make at the last church we helped, with joining them and leaving the district, was now an easy one, a no-brainer as they say, and God's peace was all over it. I had just faced the same scenario several months ago and that's why there was no peace then, because God wanted us with this new church. That door had to shut so this one could open after we served there a little longer.

With all the duties we had with this new church, because we shared space with another, and factoring in that Belinda, myself, and even the pastor worked overnights, Sunday services took a lot of effort to set up and tear down. I would have to go by the pastor's house about forty five minutes early and load up all the audio equipment, and then we'd meet at the church to get ready. Over a period of time we acquired more musicians, so setup and teardown was getting longer. It wasn't just show up for church, but hard labor before and after. Even with lack of sleep from our jobs, we all knew we were in God's plan and the burden was light. This was an exciting time in our lives as we were pillars in a starting church, with people that loved God with all their hearts too.

I would play guitar, head up the audio/visual, and preach occasionally. This felt so good, and the thoughts and prayers of a dream a few months ago, was now our next walk of faith. The prayer I prayed was answered - the thought that we may not have any more opportunities to serve was shattered - the next door in the hallway was opened and we walked in - all of the ministry experiences, tests, and walks we had trod, led up to what I was now thinking was our landing pad. Yes, I felt that after about fourteen years of touch-and-go's that we finally landed. I remember trying to explain it to the pastors, and even though they seemed excited to hear it, I couldn't express in words exactly how it made me feel, and to this day, I still can't. It was like a very heavy burden was lifted off of me and for once in our lives, we knew we were home. We landed!

As much as I didn't want to keep that overnight stocking job, I believe God had me there for a season and a reason. It didn't take long for the favor of the Lord to promote me to an assistant store manager. They approached me before and I immediately turned down the offer, but then they asked again and I said I couldn't take the position unless I was paid a certain amount, and I had to be off on Sunday's. I know it was God behind it because He gave me the money figure and the courage to demand it. Then when they accepted the terms, I had confirmation that that was where I needed to be for a while. I also had benefits and the ability to make bonuses, and by God's grace I did make bonuses regularly. God was increasing our storehouse for both Belinda and myself. With her bonuses too we were back on top again of our finances, and instead of living in the land of lack, we were starting to move into the land of abundance, and on top of that, our tithes were going into the zip code we lived in. Look at God!

We stepped out in faith to move back to Florida and struggled for a few years but got clean from our credit being tarnished because of the bankruptcy. We were building credit again and our scores were climbing, much quicker than they said it would. Through it all, God knew our hearts desire and that we wanted to be back with our family, and He worked it all out. He had the plan and we were in it. It may have seemed like our desire at first, but it was actually His desire all along. He has plans for all of us, and it's all dependent upon our willingness to go after them for them to come to pass. I don't even want to think where we'd be if we didn't step out in faith and trust Him all these years.

Now, Peter in the Bible had a few tests he had to endure. Some he created on his own. Growing pains you could say, and he didn't always pass them. In fact, he failed some miserably, but they were all with good intent: walking on the water in which he sank - rebuking Jesus about prophesying His death and resurrection, and then being called Satan - wanting to build three tabernacles, but was silenced by God's voice, and then was told by Jesus to keep quiet about it until He arose - asked if seven times to forgive his brother was the maximum amount, but then found out he had to multiply it by seventy - was asked to watch and pray but fell asleep three times in a row - cut the ear off the high priest's servant to protect Jesus, only to be told to put his sword away - said he would never be made to stumble because of Jesus, but then denied Him three times the very same night.

As we learned in Scripture, Peter didn't let those things keep him down long, but he learned from them and kept going. Jesus' ultimate plan for him was that he would be the rock that the church would be built on (Ref. Mat. 16:18). Tests from God shape us and mold us. They all have a purpose and it's up to us what to do with the test scores afterwards, whether we pass or fail. In life, we may not always do things perfectly the first time, and God knows that, but He still uses it for His plans for us. I think God had us go through some tests for this very reason too. We certainly didn't pass all of them, but we learned and kept going.

Imagine the turmoil Peter must have went through after denying Jesus and witnessing His death. Then after Jesus rising back up, the awkwardness and humility he experienced until Jesus addressed it and forgave him, and then being commissioned to feed the sheep (Ref. John 21). Yes, Peter went through a period of regrets and ashamedness, but through it all, he still obeyed Jesus to follow Him.

When Peter asked Jesus to bid that he come and walk on the water, Jesus already knew how it would turn out, but still He said to Peter, "Come" in Matthew chapter 14. Jesus could have just said, "there's no sense in trying Peter, you're just going to fail." - "this is not going to turn out like you want it to." - "you are setting yourself up for disappointment." - "you are just going to embarrass yourself and be the ridicule of conversations..." Still, with Jesus knowing this, he told Peter to "come".

At first, it looked like Peter was going to make it as he started actually walking on the water, but then when he took his eyes off Jesus, and looked around and became afraid, he began to sink. The key here, and this is what I believe Peter took away from that experience, was not to dwell on the sinking's in our lives, but to remember the zeal that got us out of our boats - walking to Jesus with faith as our steppingstones, before we lost our focus by distractions.

So even though we (now I am including everyone reading this too when I say "we" or "us" in this paragraph), may have had the faith to walk on water but then sank - had good intent to help someone but had it thrown back in our faces - went through tests that we failed miserably at - done some things we were ashamed of and wished we could have taken it back or done it differently... Jesus knew all along how those things were going to turn out but still has plans for us. He's not done with "us"! But He doesn't expect us to continue to fall short, but to take the experiences, and learn and be strengthened by them. I am so glad we never gave up on serving and threw in the towel, or got so bitter we declined God's next plan for our lives, or were so blinded in self-pity that we failed to recognize that there was even a next plan.

Now, we were living in the townhome and were comfortable there, but really felt it was time to buy a house instead of paying rent. Our desire was to have a big backyard for Buddy to play in, and a place in Florida we could call home. Where we were at, had a very small yard, so most every day I would take him for a walk just so he could exercise and so I could pray. With our job situations we knew we could make the payments, but didn't have any move-in, or down payment money. After doing some praying and researching, we came to find out that we could actually withdraw Belinda's 401k to use for a house down payment with no penalties. There wasn't a whole lot accumulated in it yet, but it was a pretty good start.

We found a house for sale on a one acre parcel that we were really interested in. After seeing it, and analyzing all the work it needed, (it was a fixer-upper), we prayed and decided to put a bid in after we learned that there was a special loan that could include renovation costs and a super low down payment too. It required $1000 down, which held it for us and gave us time to investigate the repairs needed to get it back into great shape. We hired a home inspector and to our dismay, learned it needed way too much work than we first thought.

We had a lot of dreams for that house and put a lot of time and effort into planning the renovations, but after the report of the electrical being out of date and it needing a new water well, we knew we were way over our budget and over our heads. Now there was a clause in the contract that said our deposit was non-refundable, so we went to praying and God gave us favor, and praise God we were able to get our $1000 deposit back. So, our search to buy a house went on hold for a while. We did learn a lot from the process, especially about the loan that could get us into a house.

Belinda continued to search through the housing sales and came across one that caught both of our attentions. Something just felt right about it and so we went to check it out. Our son in-law had just recently got his realtor license, so it was obvious to let him represent us. His family would be blessed by the sale, it would also give him some more experience, and we could definitely trust him.

The asking price was pretty reasonable, but the house needed some repairs. The roof was old, and we could see where it had leaked before. The furnace and duct work looked like they had not changed the filter regularly, so we knew that needed attention too. We were on a tight budget, and with the new knowledge of this loan and being able to roll the repair costs into the loan, it seemed doable and felt right. A peace was over the whole thing and we knew God was putting everything in line and giving us our hearts' desires. We were still left with a deficit in our closing costs, but really trusted God was going to do it.

The same God that made a way for us to get everything else over the last few years, was the same God we felt was going to get us into this house and put a new furnace and roof on it. We sold so much stuff to come up with the down payment but still lacked, so God gave us an idea for the contract proposal. We weren't going to offer a lower price than they were asking, but God said to instead, ask for the sellers to help with our part of the closing costs. Talk about an awesome God, they accepted and didn't even try to counteroffer, so we ended up needing very little money to move in.

God had done it again! I was in awe of the whole situation and how He was moving in our lives. Once again, we had our own house keys and were homeowners. Just three years prior we started all over when moving back to Florida, and if you would have told me all of God's blessings He was going to do in that short amount of time, I honestly may not have believed it. To this day we are still living in that house and amazed at how it all came together for us to acquire it - get a new roof - a new furnace/AC unit including all new duct work - and even by many people blessing us financially with housewarming gifts to be able to paint the outside. Not only were we home, we were also home in church as well. We had finally landed!

Over the next little while Belinda had been promoted to store manager and God was showering blessings that we almost couldn't contain. But along with the promotion came a lot of extra responsibility and hours she had to put in. We barely saw each other, and the overnights were really hard on the both of us. We did have a few day shifts that we worked too, and I had stopped working for my brother's business out of the home, as working both jobs were wearing me out. Belinda was getting worn out too and we really started praying for some kind of change, but it seemed we were almost trapped at our jobs.

Belinda was starting to complain of a lower abdominal pain, and it wasn't getting any better. In fact, it was getting worse. So bad that she had to rush to the ER and get immediate surgery. What had happened is she got a hernia, and her appendix went through it choking off the blood supply which is extremely painful and rare. So, she had her appendix removed, and it was definitely a miracle it didn't erupt from what the doctor said. A month later, she had to go back for a second surgery to get her hernia repaired.

The company she worked for was not easy on her or compassionate, and still expected her to perform as she did before, and a lot of her job consisted of physical labor. Being a store manager left little time to properly rest and take care of herself, and finally one day she had enough. She came home crying, upset, and told me she walked out and quit. She just couldn't physically take it any longer and there were no light duty jobs.

I must admit I was both shocked and relieved. She had never just walked off a job before, and this was way out of character for her, so I knew she had reached her limit. I wasn't angry or disappointed, but glad to see her come to this decision. That job was a blessing financially for sure, but we had to consider her health too. She got paid a lot more than me, and we thought about how we were going to make it, but felt peace over everything and knew God was going to take care of us as He always had. Both of us were feeling that she shouldn't rush out and get a job immediately. She had accumulated more money in her 401k, and we knew that would hold us for a while, as well as tax refund time was a few months away.

During this time our son, who had just opened his own business, asked Belinda and me if we would be interested in running the online parts sales for him. It wasn't a salary or an hourly opportunity, but we would make money strictly off the profits of sales for that part of the business. We just kind of dismissed it, being that we both didn't have much experience in the field he was in. After that, we didn't give it much thought, nor did we feel that we should pursue it. So, it went way back on the backburner and we told him we would consider it, but more than likely our answer would be no.

There was a new year quickly on us and we just made it through the Christmas season. The church we were at always did a 21 day Daniel fast at the beginning of the year, and we were excited to start it. It was going to start after a New Year's revival that another ministry was hosting. Belinda and I couldn't make it to the first service, but after hearing the report from our pastor how accurate the prophet's ministry was, we knew we needed to be there, and that maybe God had a word for us too.

The first service we could attend was powerful, and the prophet had called up couples in ministry so he could pray for them. So, we went up and he was speaking into the lives of many. Now this was in no way new to us, as this was the kind of ministry we were trained under when we were on the road for years. So, we felt like we were at home in that place. When he finally got to us, I had no idea what was going to be spoken but was thinking maybe it was just going to be confirmation to what we've always heard. That God called us together as a couple - that He was going to use us in ministry together - that I had a preachers call on my life - that Belinda had a call and a prayer ministry... but the words that were spoken took me to my knees.

I had never heard those words prophesied over me before, and the presence of God was so strong that I just started uncontrollably weeping. I couldn't tell you if Belinda got ministered to, or if she did, what was spoken over her. All I know is God spoke through the prophet very specifically to me, and the words pierced my spirit like nothing has before. So, I wrote down what was said afterwards, that "there is an anointing on me with numbers, and with digits. That He will even cause me to inherit a business. And that He will cause me to "do" a business". What all that meant at the time, I had no clue.

There were other specific things spoken about ministry work too, and some of the words seemed kind of odd. So even with not knowing how such things could happen (as we almost always seem to wonder), I pondered on them and felt in my spirit a powerful belief in them, and a knowledge and assurance that they would come to pass. My spirit had ignited, and I was in anticipation to what God was going to be doing in the next chapter of our lives. The church we were at sparked a refreshing, and the 21 day fast was in place. Even many prophecies went over it and our pastors. We had gone through New Year's fasts and revivals, but this one was probably one of the most memorable.

Belinda was still out of work, and with no release for her to search for employment, God was miraculously meeting our needs as He always had. We didn't have much insight into what He was going to do next, but the same peace that was on us in the other walks of faith was present in our lives. I was making good money at my job and made bonuses regularly. Then, God started to have me ponder the idea of our son's proposal, about helping his business. I had not thought about it at all for months, so I prayed and sought Him on it. What we had dismissed so quickly before, started to really be impressed upon me. Belinda and I discussed it further and thought that maybe it could be good for her and help our income some. We knew our son didn't have a lot of credit, but we had just paid off one of our credit cards recently and thought we could use it for the business to buy parts with and then resell them.

The business was still pretty much at its infancy and had potential for growth. As the background, our son was known in the automotive market with calibrating, or tuning is what it's called, car and truck computers for high performance. The business he started branched off of previous companies he worked for, but he had this idea that his last boss didn't take an interest in for a certain type of tune unlike anything else on the market.

I remember when he started it, he was living with us at the time, and had already quit his job, and was at the kitchen table working one day on his laptop writing tunes for trucks and selling a few of them. Then he shared with us how his idea was now a reality. He had sat at the table for over eleven hours and like a light bulb going on, he figured out how to program this tune to operate in a revolutionary new way. The boss that thought he was crazy for the idea, was now proven wrong, and I remember our son giving God credit for the wisdom behind figuring it out.

So, Belinda and I were seriously considering the parts business now. The more we prayed about it the more we felt led to pursue it. It was going to be a risk for us with our personal credit backing things up for inventory, but from what we were learning about the possibility for sales, it seemed more like a God idea. I always say there are good ideas, and then there are God ideas. Good ideas come and go, but God ideas stick! As I said back in chapter 2 as well, "God ideas have an assurance and peace, even though they may contradict everything surrounding it". But I would like to add here the contrast, that good ideas come with apprehensions and fear. So, with the peace we were feeling, we knew it was a God idea, and everybody in the family and church was liking the fact that maybe Belinda could just work from the house and not have to get a retail job again.

We ordered our initial buy in with one of our first distributors, which was over $2000 and immediately sold a few of the products. I must say I was a little nervous about putting our own money up, but in the spirit I felt good. We opened another account with one of the top automotive aftermarket parts suppliers, and also with a few other companies that God gave us favor with. Belinda and I started adding parts to the website, and before long we had a fair number of products. I had taken a week off of work because I had to use the time up, but mostly to continue to add parts to the website. Most of them we didn't have to keep in stock, but we could drop ship them from our suppliers.

So, in a fairly short period of time we had the parts department up and going.

We weren't making a whole lot of money but were starting to see the potential our son had talked about. Belinda was able to stay at home now, as our income was supplemented by this new venture that God had put together. So, after a few months, and with the business starting to grow slowly, God reminded me of the prophecy at the beginning of the year in which He said, "He will cause me to do a business". It was happening. I didn't understand at the time the word that was spoken into my life, or even imagined it coming to pass so quickly, but there we were, doing a business. As I have said before, "God NEVER ever ceases to amaze me, but after all, He is God".

Every free moment I had was spent trying to grow the business. We had to learn about website design - creating spreadsheets to keep track of the books - learn about an industry we knew very little about - become educated on all the parts we sold and all the applications - interacted on social media to drive sales - even learned some about the complicated tuning that our son had been doing for a dozen years or so. But it was beginning to look like for the parts department to really take off, that I would have to put 100% of my time into it.

So, I went into praying and seeking God for direction. I was praising Him and was so humbled that a prophecy that was released over my life just a short time ago, would already be in place. Not that I had doubts, but my experience with a prophetic word, or even the seed of a thought God placed into my spirit, usually turned out to be an early preview before the long awaited release. Sometimes, even years would go by before things fell into place. Just like when I thought about what it must be like to serve in the full time ministry at the plant I worked at, and then three or four years later it happened.

I sometimes think people get ahead of God when they hear a word spoken over them. I have been guilty of that for sure. I mean, we know God has plans, but we may either intentionally or unintentionally take matters into our own hands. We may know where we are heading to, and instead of trusting the Holy Ghost GPS He has for us, we turn it off and start driving the route we want or think we should go. We either rush into things or delay them.

For Belinda and myself to get to where we are in ministry and life, we had to get hurt - veer off course - had to have isolation - had to leave our family and go on the road - had to sell out and up-and-move to a new city a few times - had to change jobs... but the main thing we had to do was to live and breathe our trust in Him. To place it all in His hands and leave it there. Definitely not the easiest thing to do as it takes conditioning and persistence. It starts out slow and kind of easy, and then it gets to be more intense, like a longer workout. But the more you do it, the easier it gets. Not easier as far as stretching your faith, but easier to hand off the responsibilities of planning, and entrusting them to Him.

So, as I was working my full time job, and was able to pray on my overnight shifts when I was at the store by myself for a few hours here and there, and I would ask God what he wanted us to do. I felt just like at the plant I worked at twenty years ago, that my job was starting to come to an end after being there for about five years. I felt apprehension but also expectation. It would be a huge step of faith to quit another good paying job with benefits to venture to the unknown. Now, I just heard a preacher say that there are risk-takers, and then there are faith walkers, but I had never thought any of our walks were risks. I didn't really analyze them and weight things out, but just followed His leading and His peace went with it.

I knew for this business that God had given us to really take off and be successful, I was going to have to go at it full time. Just a few hours a week just wasn't enough. I had another week of vacation due, so I took it, and Belinda and I worked long hours every day that I was off to build the website and learn. God's peace and favor was over our lives and I felt strong to put in my two weeks' notice when I went back to work and I did. I must say those weeks didn't go by quick enough.

From the time I received the prophecy about doing a business, to the time I left my job was seven months. God was quickly moving, and this is where the walk of faith really started. We were still serving in the church He landed us at, and it felt really great to have a "normal" work schedule and not have to work overnight shifts any longer, but now our income was solely dependent upon parts sales. I cashed in my 401k and that held us over for a bit, but we were praying everything in just to make ends meet.

I must admit there were a few times to where my heart caved in because of slow business, and this was just a few months into things. I knew we were in God's will, but the flesh side of me would show up and show out, and Belinda would catch me weeping because of the stress of slow sales. We had gotten so comfortable with our day jobs that we had forgotten what it was like to live by faith again. It's easy to have faith when you know you are getting a paycheck every week, but take that away, that's where faith really kicks in. It was a roller coaster of emotions and I had to constantly remind myself that God would provide and get us through. We didn't want anyone to know how bad it was getting financially as our bills were starting to get paid a little late, but they were getting paid.

It was almost getting to the point of, "what were we thinking!?", but the faith we had inside knew God was going to somehow get us through, even if we had to make sacrifices and go backwards first to get ahead. I kept remembering the prophecies and how God said it was going to happen. We didn't rush God on this venture or get ahead or behind His timing for it. We had to pull out all restraints for that I assure you. We just watched as He orchestrated everything to take place exactly like He planned, which was far different than we could have imagined.

Chapter 11
The Storm

L iving in Florida says you can expect hurricanes, and this year was no different than any other. Just two months after I left my job, Irma's path was heading straight towards us, and projected to be a Category 2 in strength. We had prepared like we always did, but with little money we couldn't get much supplies. The stores had already been picked through, and the quickly emptied shelves made it look like they were going out of business. It was kind of scary how quickly they ran out, but we knew no matter what, God would take care of us. Now, this wasn't our first hurricane, and being inland gave a better chance for less damage, but we never had a Cat 2 hurricane at our front door, so we cleaned out our walk-in closet and made our shelter and got into it with our two Doberman's, Buddy and Maggie.

We weren't but just a few hours into the major part of the storm approaching and our power went out. We had flashlights and my cell phone so we could still monitor things, and it weakened some to a Cat 1 before the eye reached us. The devastation it left behind completely wiped out some towns, and the power outages were almost statewide. Our son and our daughter hadn't lost power and offered for us to come over to one of their places, but we thought we'd ride it out. Plus, Buddy was a senior dog now and had some health issues, and we thought it would be too hard on him, so we decided just to stay put because we had the big backyard which they didn't have. He couldn't do walks like he used to do, so staying home was the best option..

Everything in the fridge and freezer were lost because ice was nowhere to be found, even if you could find a store with power, they were sold out of ice. Structurally our house was untouched, except for just a few tree limbs in the yard. Our roof was fine too because we had put a new one on when we bought the place, but there were lots of houses in the neighborhood that had missing shingles and had to put tarps on theirs. So, after almost five days of no power and the temperatures in the nineties, power was restored. The worst part about it for us, besides the Summer heat, is that we weren't able to work without power and internet, which hindered us making much money that week.

In the natural, I wasn't really sure what we were going to do about our income. This was a leap of faith and the bills weren't going to go away, but we knew God had directed us thus far. Then we heard on the news about FEMA disaster relief for Florida homes that were directly impacted by the hurricane, so I went to their website to see if we qualified for any kind of help. Even though our house wasn't damaged, there were still questions about loss of food and power being out for an extended period of time. I filled out the application and didn't get an immediate approval, but it said our case would go under further review. So, it looked like we didn't qualify for any assistance, nor were we really expecting any because we came out unscathed.

Business was starting to get a little bit better, but still not where we needed it to be. We then found out that even the loan companies were offering hurricane assistance, so we checked into them for our car and house. Turned out that we could defer our car payment for two months, and that they would just put the two payments on the back end of the loan. That was great news because it gave us a few months to breathe on that bill. Then with our home mortgage, they offered a ninety day forbearance program that we could pay whatever we could but had to make up all the payments before the end of it. That way even if we got a little behind for a few months, our home couldn't go into foreclosure, and wouldn't get reported to the credit agencies as being in default.

We were so grateful, and it gave us some time to really press into the business, plus the Christmas shopping season was coming up and we hoped sales would pick up then. We knew the money was going to stay tight for a while, but now we had some much needed relief from the stress we were under. Now I had mentioned before about unexpected checks in the mail when we first moved back to Florida, but this trip to the mailbox left me speechless and overwhelmed. There was a check from FEMA for $1002. It took me by surprise so much that I had to call them to make sure there wasn't a mistake, and there wasn't. It was legit. I am praising God all over again just writing this! That money came at the exact right time to get us through a little further.

We also found out that the Food Stamp assistance place was giving out a one-time voucher to those that lost food because of power outages, even if they were not already getting benefits or could not previously qualify for help. So, I went to their website to apply and it looked like we made too much money the month of, and the month after the hurricane came through; as I had to factor in the FEMA check also for our income. I hit the backspace on the form and changed our numbers to see how much we missed it by, and it was only $8. So, I went back again and changed the numbers back to what I originally had. I didn't have any intentions of beating the system, not even for $8, although I may have been tempted for a second. So, I submitted the form anyways knowing we didn't qualify for help and trusted that God would honor our honesty.

The Food Stamps deadline for claiming hurricane benefits was quickly approaching, and the pastor's wife asked if we had gone down in person to talk to them. I told her about our situation and that we didn't qualify, and she shared with us how she knew a few people that went down and talked to them in person and got the one-time benefit. I kind of dismissed it again and thought it would be just a waste of my time and theirs, not to mention the thought of embarrassment to even try and still get denied. But every time we saw her, she asked if we'd gone yet, and I still felt like it wasn't worth all the effort. She was adamant that even if we didn't qualify, that if we went and explained our situation about losing electricity and food, that maybe they would help like the other people she knew that got help.

I've never been the kind of person to rush to an assistance place for a handout, I'm too proud for that, but after her constant urging for us to go, we went. Now, because of the expected turnout it was held at a shopping mall. We got there fairly early and the parking lot was packed. The lines started on the outside and it was like a maze on the inside. I have never seen such a thing. It was standing room only, and the lines weaved up and down the wings of the mall like waiting in line at an amusement park but magnified.

It took hours for us to finally get to the huge vacant department store space, and there were numerous tables with workers on laptops doing the prescreening. It was finally our turn and they took my information, studied the screen for a second, raised their eyebrows, and then told me we had to go to a holding area until someone came to get us. There was only one other person there and I had a very bad feeling and was starting to prepare for embarrassment. A few minutes later someone came and escorted all of us down and around the crowds to another holding area and told us to wait until someone called us. This place wasn't as big as the one we came from, but there were still a lot of workers on laptops.

They kept on calling names and the wait was still pretty long, and the one person that was escorted in with us said something like he was wasting his time and was going to get denied anyways, and just got up and left. I was starting to think the same thing too, but Belinda felt we just needed to wait. So, the person that was in charge of calling names and directing people to the workers had to go on break. It must have been their supervisor that relieved them because she started speeding up the process and was walking around with an iPad questioning those waiting.

She finally came around to us and I was as honest as I could be, explaining that when I submitted the online application I hit the backspace on the form and changed our numbers to see how much we missed it by, and it was only $8. But that I went back again to change the numbers back to what I originally had before hitting the submit button. Also, that I didn't have any intentions of beating the system, I was just curious. Then I explained to her how we heard that even though the online process denied benefits, that people were getting help by coming down in person.

She didn't seem to be concerned about none of that but asked me several questions about how we were affected by the hurricane. Asked if we lost power and for how long. Asked if we lost food and an approximate dollar amount in losses. She then signaled to one of the workers on the laptops and motioned to them that I was going to be next. After she walked me over, she said something to them and gave them instructions. It was then that I knew with certainty that she was a supervisor.

So, after spending half a day there I finally felt like we were going to be leaving soon, and quite possibly empty handed still. The worker asked for my information and pulled me up on the computer. They then asked another worker sitting by them a question, and both of them were viewing my information on the screen looking a little bewildered. I was handed a piece of paper and was asked to sign it. It was then I realized we had gotten approved and we received two months' worth of benefits. It was extremely hard for me to see as we walked out because I was teary-eyed knowing that God had moved for us. I believe God placed that supervisor there at that very time just for me. I didn't see her again, and the worker she relieved was now back. It could have turned out far differently if that worker didn't go on break when she did. Once again, God made provisions for us, gave us favor, and it was in His perfect timing. God ALWAYS amazes me, and it NEVER gets old!

We were so blessed to be able to "do" this business as the prophet of God spoke, and the next few months were trying as money was still very tight, but with all the assistance we got, we were doing it. I don't think we shared with many people how rough it was, as there was really no reason to because we knew God was moving for us. We just didn't want anyone to feel sorry for us or give any negative criticisms like maybe we were taking too great a risk and possibly could lose our house and car. We didn't even let our son know, and it was his business, as we didn't want to put any extra stress on him anyways.

Sometimes we have to remain silent in our faith walks and just let God do what He does without letting any outside influence in. Our nature is to tell people and share what's going on, but in doing so we allow their thoughts and opinions to enter in. I'm not saying it's a bad thing, but it's not a healthy thing. We have to protect our faith, what we know and believe, and shield out all the drama that could be a hindrance. Even believers of like faith whom we trust could unknowingly interject a seed of doubt that could easily sprout up and take over our garden of faith. So, it's best to remain silent and let God do God, unless He specifically tells us to share with others.

The next few months were easier than the previous ones as business was picking up, but now we were facing the Christmas shopping Holiday, our car payments were starting back up, the Food Stamps benefits were all used up, and also we were needing to come up with enough in mortgage payments to not go into default. The good news was that tax season was right around the corner, and we were now also into the Black Friday through Christmas period. God amazed us with really great sales, and it was definitely the financial boost we needed, but we were still lacking to get our mortgage caught up.

Now we strongly believe in God's principles of sowing and reaping, and felt as we went into this new year, we needed to sow a financial seed for our personal finances and the business. In the natural, you just don't take the money that you need and spend it, but I believe in sowing it. We had so many times over the years sacrificially sowed into the Kingdom, and every time God never let our finances collapse because of it.

Belinda felt strongly to sow $218 for 2018 which was a lot of money - money that we needed - money that was hard to let go of - but we knew as before that He would honor it. So in faith, we sowed that seed as we had many other times over the previous twenty years, just like as the Bible says in 2 Corinthians 9:6-8, *"But this I say: He who sows sparingly will also reap sparingly, and he who sows bountifully will also reap bountifully. So, let each one give as he purposes in his heart, not grudgingly or of necessity; for God loves a cheerful giver. And God is able to make all grace abound toward you, that you, always having all sufficiency in all things, may have an abundance for every good work"*.

It wasn't long after that, as the deadline for meeting our mortgage agreement to get caught up in payments was approaching, some dear friends of ours handed us an envelope. Now, we in no way solicited handouts, or shared our financial situation with anyone, or expressed that we were lacking or needing help, so we knew this had to be God! Inside the envelope was ten one hundred dollar bills. They said God had told them to give it to us, and it was extremely needed and came at the perfect time. I was teary eyed, shocked, and at a loss for words; and at the same time in my mind, I was dancing in the Spirit and jumping and praising God. We were getting so much closer to getting caught up, and this was a huge, huge impact.

Our tax return came out really good and we were getting down to the wire, as the last few months prior were probably some of the hardest we had ever endured with all the financial weight on us. Amazingly, all fell into His perfect alignment to help with catching up the mortgage payments, and we got back on top of things financially. We were in awe. We knew He was going to do it, but He had stretched us like He never had before. The enemy intensely played with my mind throughout the time I left my full-time job up to that point, but I did it. I pressed through, shook off doubt when it arose, and solely depended on God to fulfill what He deposited into my spirit.

Now I can't speak for Belinda, but I felt like I just ran an eight month marathon through the hardest of obstacles, both mentally and spiritually; with God splitting the Red Sea for us to make it to the other side, narrowly escaping Pharaoh and his army from trying to enslave us and drag us back to Egypt. Well, maybe not quite like that, but I know the devil didn't want us to succeed in this business venture and he put up a hard, hard fight.

As I have looked back through all that happened and how everything came together, I can see God every step of the way. Precisely using time and events to work out for our good. Had it not been the right timing for me to quit my job to put 100% of our time into the business, and for a hurricane to come through central Florida when it did, we may very well have lost our house and car. Now I know many did lose homes and cars because of the impact of the storm, and it's definitely heartbreaking, but I feel we would have lost everything anyways not even being storm related with our finances crashing. But God used a hurricane to our favor, because if it had not come, and events didn't happen the way they did:

- We wouldn't have been able to get our car payment deferred for two months.
- We wouldn't have had the opportunity for our mortgage to go into forbearance, protecting us from foreclosure and bad credit reporting.
- FEMA would not have sent us a thousand and two dollars.
- The Food Stamps place would not have given us two months' worth of benefits to feed us.
- I believe our financial seed we sowed moved God's hand, with us having the obedience and faith to sow it, which I believe was critical in His plans. The little bit we had went further in God's hand than it ever could have went in ours. I believe it caused God to speak to our friends to bless us with a thousand dollars.
- And then lastly, for Tax refund season to be right near the end of the mortgage forbearance to get us totally caught up.

All of this got us through and gave us the chance to build the business enough to where it could start to sustain us. Also, we faithfully tithed the profits that we made from our end of the business, no matter how much or how little we made, and I believe that was key to God's blessings on it. Now, I don't want to be redundant here or quickly rush through this, but I must say it again in a slightly different way, God used a storm and turned it around for our good, and to our favor. There is no way anyone can say it was luck, or just a series of fortunate events. I saw God's hand over everything, and I think that's where some people miss it. They don't recognize or see Him moving in every aspect of their lives. Even in life's storms.

Jesus said to Nicodemus in John 3:3, "*Most assuredly, I say to you, unless one is born again, he cannot see the kingdom of God.*" That word "see" in the original language means to experience. God's kingdom isn't meant to be some mysterious, unreachable thing, it's meant to be seen and experienced. Right now! In this life, not the next. He then goes on and says in verse 11, "*Most assuredly, I say to you, We speak what We know and testify what We have seen, and you do not receive Our witness*". Jesus was telling him there is a difference in knowing about the kingdom of God and experiencing it. When you experience it, you testify what you have seen. You are in it. When you only know about it, you are not connected, but only have assumptions.

We can experience, or see, the Kingdom of God daily. All we have to do is look, because nothing in the Kingdom of God happens by chance. But everything is on purpose, and for a purpose. That supervisor at the Food Stamp place took over when she did at that time for a purpose. Pastor's wife kept insisting that we'd go there for a purpose. I quit my job when I did for a purpose… and numerous other things in my life that I know God influenced. I may not have seen all of them with my physical eyes, but saw them with my spiritual eyes, and experienced the Kingdom of God through them all.

Someone maybe thinking now that we just got lucky, or possibly our own efforts got us through. That maybe it was just our time to win. That nothing ever good happens to them, but it does for everyone else. I may have thought that too a few times in my early walk with Jesus, but I personally heard from many others their witness, and it elevated my faith that God could do the same for us. And I not only heard their witness, but also celebrated with them, without jealousy. Jesus told Nicodemus *"you do not receive Our witness"*. He wasn't asking a question either, He was making a bold statement. Nicodemus couldn't experience the Kingdom of God because he couldn't believe Their testimony.

Now I know that Jesus was talking about being born again in those verses, and I am assuming most reading this are already are saved, but the question is, are we trusting the Holy Spirit to move for us even though we can't tell where He is coming from or where He is going with our situation? Jesus said a very profound statement in John 3:8, *"The wind blows where it wishes, and you hear the sound of it, but cannot tell where it comes from and where it goes. So is everyone who is born of the Spirit"*. When we are born of the Spirit there is a tangible presence felt, we can actually hear Him, like hearing the effects of the wind, blowing in our lives.

Now, the natural wind cannot be heard unless it is impacting something. It has to come in contact and drag across an object like trees, water, buildings, our ears... Otherwise, we never hear it. The spiritual winds are almost constantly moving in our lives, but to feel or experience them, we need to get into their paths and feel them, and hear them. When that hurricane came, along with the many others we were in over the years, powerful winds came with them. I remember opening a door and hearing the howling wind, feeling the strong gusts, and an awkward pressure in my head from it. If I had never done that, I would not have fully experienced it. But I did, and I felt the forces. Which was probably poor judgement for certain with opening a door in a hurricane. Sure, I could hear it from the inside of the house but opening the door and poking my head out took me into the fullness of it.

Before I got saved, I knew about Jesus - knew about his miracles - knew all the stories of His power - but until I actually jumped in and entered the kingdom of God, I never saw Him move in my life. He was in control of everything, and as I looked back over my life, I can now see Him in many situations, I just never realized it. Jesus used the wind as an illustration of the work of the Holy Spirit in John 3:8, and as the wind seemingly "blows where it wishes", so the Holy Spirit sovereignly works. He cannot be controlled, and He works in ways we cannot predict or understand. He cannot be fully understood, but the proof of His work is apparent. Where the Holy Spirit works, there is undeniable and unmistakable evidence.

The many walks of faith Belinda and I have traveled were just as Jesus illustrated here. We couldn't always tell which way the wind was going to blow - couldn't always understand where it was He was taking us to - nor did we know how or by what means He was going to take us - we just listened for the wind (the Holy Spirit) and got in contact with Him. So many just let the Holy Spirit blow around them and never get into His path. They know He's out there and can see the effects, but they never get so intrigued with all the commotion and just open the door in the hurricane, but instead, intentionally or not, get into their innermost room of the house to try to escape Him. I know I've been guilty.

To go back a few verses in that passage of scripture to John 3:5, *"Jesus answered, "Most assuredly, I say to you, unless one is born of water and the Spirit, he cannot enter the kingdom of God"*. There is no way, like Nicodemus, that we can experience and partake of all that God has for us in the kingdom of God here on this Earth, unless we get Spiritually minded and listen for the direction the Spirit is taking us to. We can very easily (talking spiritually here), stay inside with the doors and windows closed in the comfort of our lives, or we can go out to where the winds are blowing and see where they take us to and get out of our comfort zones, and get into the Comforter's zone. See what He has for us, and experience and "see" the kingdom of God Jesus spoke about in John 3:3.

Nicodemus was a very educated, religious man, but a strong desire in him had to get to Jesus, and Jesus explained to him that there was so much more, and that there was an experience he was missing out on. Nicodemus was looking at things in the natural realm and wanted more. Jesus wants the same for us too. We can have the ability to see, or experience the Kingdom of God, right where we are at. Right now! And did we ever see God move like the wind in our trials. We didn't know how he was going to move for us, only that He was.

Paul taught us in 1 Cor. 2:14, and I love the Amplified Version of this, *"But the natural, nonspiritual man does not accept or welcome or admit into his heart the gifts and teachings and revelations of the Spirit of God, for they are folly (meaningless nonsense) to him; and he is incapable of knowing them [of progressively recognizing, understanding, and becoming better acquainted with them] because they are spiritually discerned and estimated and appreciated".* I pray that no one is like how this describes, being cold to the Spirit of God, and shunning off God's gifts as being meaningless. But that is how the natural mind thinks, and I include myself as thinking that way in the past. It's not a matter of just changing your mindset, but a matter of actually knowing God. Not just to know about Him, but to know Him through His Word and prayer. We can then see with spiritual eyes, and accept, welcome, and admit in our hearts; the gifts, teachings, and revelations of God.

When I first started my job stocking overnights, it was overwhelming the number of boxes, and trying to figure out where everything went. All I saw was a forest of trees. Everything just blended together. There was no distinction between things. No sense of order in my mind to where everything went or how it all fit together to make up something I could comprehend. It was all just one-dimensional.

The more I was there though - the more I got used to my surroundings - became more familiar with how everything was laid out - how things were organized in the stockroom - what were in all the boxes, and how I could more easily find products by recognizing the box and not having to read the label - how many individual items made up a section of the store - how they were organized to make it easier for shoppers to find products... the one big blob of trees was starting to look more like pine trees, redwoods, a group of maples, oaks... I was seeing the sparrows, robins, owls, hawks... insects, snakes, worms, beetles... Ivy, weeds, ferns, moss… What looked like a forest at first, was now starting to look like a kingdom in a sense. I was starting to see the forest, and how it was made up of thousands of individual, unique things. Everything had a purpose and played an important part of making it all up.

The more I walk with God, read His word, and pray fervently, the more I can see how intricate He is. When I first envisioned the Kingdom of God, what I saw was me standing way off at a distance, kind of like looking at a forest and only seeing a dense group of trees. But now I can see myself actually in the forest, gazing around and admiring how it is all made up. I see myself becoming more familiar with it and learning the pathways and discovering all the habitat there. No more walking in fear but walking in peace. Exploring every day and no longer feeling like a stranger, but more like a resident. I may not be an expert or a park ranger yet, but I can now find my way around and recognize certain things. It's my neighborhood and I belong there.

I can recognize God in my situations now - see His hand of deliverance - notice when He aligns events - understand better when things don't go my way and know He has a better plan - I praise Him in times of trials, knowing and trusting all things work together for the good - I can see that what the enemy means or meant for evil, God is going to use it for good - I can trust He will protect me and always has my best interest - that He hears my prayers and knows my heart's desires - that He has a purpose and plans for me - that no matter how bad I mess up or miss the mark, He is still there with an outstretched hand - that if I fully give my life into His bosom, He will hold me close and show me great and mighty things I know yet not - that if He speaks and I move in obedience, He will fulfill what He has promised!

Chapter 12
Back In Flight

T he money roller coaster ride was finally over for us, and it was a huge sigh of relief, as we were feeling stability in our finances once again. God's hand directly worked out what looked like the impossible for us. Every day I stand in amazement, and also in humbleness with what He did then, now, and all throughout our lives. I KNOW how much HE has blessed us. Yes, it was Him. Not by our own power or by luck that we are where we are now, and I also know that He holds it altogether too. With every fiber of my being I try not to get wrapped up in all the blessings and forget the source from which it all comes from, knowing just like Job, as the Lord gives, He can also take away. (Ref. Job 1:21)

What I have noticed, being we have lived both in the lands of lack as well as the lands of abundance, is that I sometimes strayed from Him when I didn't have much lack. When everything was going OK, I spent less communion time with Him. Not intentionally, but the enemy slyly came in and pulled my prayer time away from me. It's like there were no urgent needs, so my prayer time was less intense, and what happened is I fell into a trap of praying less when I should have been praying the same or even greater.

So with this foreknowledge, we were focusing our prayers on other things besides finances, and I felt freedom that I hadn't felt for quite some time. The pressure of praying in money turned into thankfulness and awe. Now I can't exactly put into words the things and feelings that transpired over the next few months, but I was starting to feel that God was about to move us out of the hanger and prepare us again for flight. My heart was breaking as I was sensing this, because we absolutely loved where we were at and the people we served. I had really thought this was it! We had landed! And it was that way for many years, but I was almost double-minded, fighting with rejecting the thoughts of moving on - with facing reality that God wanted us to go back into flight. So, we hung on as long as we could, and I guess we decided not to deal with it, and just ignored God's promptings.

I mean, we didn't have anywhere else to go, nor a clue what God was wanting to do next with us. We fought with staying there with hopes that things would just work out, but they didn't. As much as God was pulling at us to leave, we were starting to feel that we were almost being pushed out of the church. Things were changing, as the friction from it was isolating us, and we felt lots of tension. Belinda and I discussed it almost every Saturday night and Sunday morning, and there was so much uneasiness surrounding us. No peace. No peace at all. When we should have been praising and praying, we were instead mumbling and complaining. Something we rarely ever did before. We tried to pray through and even fasted a few times, but still no peace if we should stay there, and it lasted for months. But deep inside we already knew the solution.

I didn't like what we were becoming and how we felt torn all the time to stay or go. We really tried to put in 100% effort, but it was hard because we were disheartened, and it really bothered us. It was getting stressful, and the dreams to stay at this church were shattered. I may have even gotten upset with God a few times because I didn't want to move on and start all over again. But as usual, as much as we can fight against God, in my case, He always wins eventually. Because I'd rather be hurt for a short time and in His will, than being miserable out of His will. I have learned over the years too, that it's much easier to quickly run the road of obedience, no matter how hard it is, than to resist, and later trudge the road of regrets. I don't know why we didn't use that wisdom then.

During my prayer time on a Sunday morning, God showed me a quick vision which solidified our decision to leave, and that we didn't need to prolong it any longer. We had been delaying it long enough already. What He showed me was Belinda and myself inside of a church (no particular one), and I saw God's hand reach inside of it and picked us up with His thumb and fingers, then gently carried us away. Almost like how you'd see someone pick a doll out of a dollhouse. We were so tiny and the Hand that carried us was humongous. So much peace overcame me like I hadn't felt in such a long time, and I wept. I knew we were attending our last service there that day, and the anguish I had been burdened with was relieved by that vision.

Also, in my prayer time, God quickly led me down memory lane. As He took me back, He gave me revelation that every ministry we had helped was for a season. Ordained for a set time by Him. Now I always cried to Him "why?" after every one ended, and I never got an answer until that morning. I had always thought it was for various reasons, blaming the church, blaming ourselves... but God told me it's because we were helps, given to a ministry to serve with them. Planted by Him and not by man. He dropped us in to fill in the gaps, to learn, and to be an encouragement. That's why doors opened so easily.

We heard from many churches that we were God-sends, but even though we had gotten deeply planted, He eventually pressed upon us that the seasons were over, and here we were again at the end of another season. This time a very long one at that; one we really thought would never end. It didn't turn out how we imagined, but really none of them did. Our assignments ended, the doors that were opened to us closed, and we were left with both fulfillment and emptiness. What once looked like a bunch of ups and downs in ministry, were actually time frames and travels God had set up for us. Walks of faith. It felt like though, that we were kind of like what I sometimes call, nomads for Jesus. Wanderers with no permanent abode taking care of sheep. But He spoke that morning that we weren't wandering at all, just following His plans.

Now starting over in ministry is painstakingly hard and very emotional, as we have had to do it many times over in following His will the last 18 years prior to that, but God reminded me that He always had and will have another plan for us. It has been over a year now since we left, and He really hasn't pushed us to get out and seek another church yet. In the vision, I saw Him carry us away, but I never saw Him lowering us back down. Belinda said she felt that God wanted us to take a long rest from serving so that I could focus more on writing, and I have. So, at this point, I am not really sure the direction He wants us to fly, we are just experiencing the flight and anticipating the next landing.

As mentioned in the opening of this book, I have seen so many people with life plans that were pursued with great passion, and gotten jealous of them, but if I had that, I would not have had these precious walks with Him. I used to kind of believe He purposely let me wander through careers, but really I know now that He was leading me all along to get me to where I am, and He is still leading me. He has blessed my hands immensely with all the jobs I have had over the years. All of them equipped me in some way to serve in the Kingdom here on Earth.

We go through life sometimes not knowing why we are where we are at, but God does. We may be there to learn or to be an influence in someone else's life, and the spiritual seeds that we are either gathering or spreading along the way, is all for His purpose; for our lives, and the lives of others. I think back to the plant I worked at, and the older Christian man that made a heavy impact in my life before I got saved. That seed grew inside of me to where I could be the older Christian man in a plant about ten years later spreading seeds. Never would I have planned for that, but God knew.

He knew that the seed that was planted, when the thought first surfaced in my mind about my first pastor serving full time in ministry - how it would sprout to where I would be serving full time in ministry one day. How the seeds of music would grow. How the seeds of audio engineering would flourish in my life one day for His Kingdom, along with many other gifts he Has blessed me with.

Now, we may think we have gone through hell on Earth sometimes, as I have been in jobs I hated but was thankful for -

I have been in life's ups and downs - been hurt by people - been hurt in ministry - I've had to let dreams go to the side - I've had to forget about the things I wanted, to get the things I needed - I've had to let go and let God be God, as much as I wanted to be in control - I've had to walk through the empty, lonely hallways not knowing what door was going to open next, or even if a door would open... but all of those trials either planted a seed or sprouted a seed.

You see, for a seed to be planted, the ground has to be first broken and worked. It needs to be prepared. The lonely breakthrough seed that was planted when I was in my deepest depression and in bondage to oppression, (when I was broken), helps me when I feel like I am going downhill. It starts to sprout, and I remember Whom I serve and that He can get me out. The just-getting-by seed that was planted when I didn't know if we were going to be homeless or not a few times in our lives, (when I was broken), sprouts when the bills get piled up, and reminds me God is my provider, and just like He did it in the past, He will do it again. The your-all-washed-up seed that was planted when I felt God was done with me in ministry, (when I was broken), pops through the soil and gives hope that life is not over, and that He still has plans for me.

Now to dig a little deeper (pun intended), a seed is dead until it gets the right combination of elements. But even though it may be dead, it carries with it a blueprint - a design that is embedded into its core – a Master's plan for it to be exactly what it was created for. An Earthly seed needs dirt, water, and the sun. Whereas a Spiritual seed needs faith, belief, and the Son. My loneliness seed, planted when I was broken in despair, contains peace and joy in the Holy Spirit. My hurt seed, planted when I was broken emotionally, contains Him who is the healer of the broken in heart. When I feel downcast and trodden on now, there is a seed containing Him who crowns us with loving-kindness and tender mercies. When the devil comes and tries his best to take me out, there is a seed containing Him who redeems my life from destruction.

We can go through life with a pocket of seeds, but until the ground gets broken, or until we ourselves get broken and those seeds are planted, they are useless. God can't plant a seed of faith until we loosen up our pride and realize that He can do more with us while we are broken, because seeds can't be sown into stony ground. He can't plant a seed of hope until all seems hopeless and we open up and invite Him in. He can't plant a seed of victory until we are victims and realize there is a more than conquerors through Him seed. He can't give us the breakthrough seed until we are tired of being broken and fully submit to His grace. He can't order our footsteps until he plants the seeds of direction, and we turn off our will and seek His.

The next seed, or the next plan can't grow until the previous one has fully flourished, and our ground is re-worked and prepared. We have to surrender fully and turn it over to Him so He can grow in us what He planted. That's what I am experiencing right now. One plan is done, and the next plan is starting to grow. It's starting to break the Earth. I will never know what it is unless I continue to water it, and I have no idea where it will take me. I just trust God and know He has another plan for us.

The most important walk of faith anyone can travel goes far greater than any walk that I wrote in this book. The one I am talking about has to happen before any walk even begins. It happened with the hall of faith patriarchs in Hebrews chapter 11, and it has to start with us too. It is trusting in the Lord. Yes, not ourselves or someone else, but in Jesus. The kind of trust which is a daily walk, not an occasional stroll. To totally trust Him with our souls - our eternal destiny - our Earthly lives - our family - our finances - our forgiveness - our healing - restoration from hurts - freedom from strongholds - to trust Him to send peace when it all feels like the sea is raging around us - trusting Him to help us pick up the pieces when we drop and shatter the precious plans He has for us. It is a commitment we make that starts out as self-discipline, but soon turns out to become a lifestyle. By trusting Him doesn't say we are weak, but it says He is stronger.

With that walk of faith, every day we expect the unexpected, good or bad. Not knowing if the battles will be fierce, or even the length of them. We just know He will be with us through every one of them. We smile on the inside, even if it doesn't show on the outside, because we feel His presence with a reassuring peace that is tangibly real; because we already know the temporary counterfeit peace that the world tries to manufacture. We have joy that envelops our inner most being, and cast asides all doubt, knowing that hopelessness will never return because we have a hope in Him. We have treasures in Him that are beyond any monetary value, and what use to seem important to us in this world, doesn't compare to the gifts He gives us through His Spirit.

Journeys in faith start by exiting off the roads you're used to while God is holding the map. As hard as it may be, conviction and trust will cause you to follow His road signs and turn down unfamiliar roads not knowing where they lead. To bring this up to today's technology, He becomes our GPS navigational device. He might even say to turn down roads that are off the beaten path. He knows where to turn. When to stop. When to go. Who to pick up and drop off. When to put the pedal down. When to cruise. When to back up. What supplies are needed for the journey. How to acquire the supplies.... and more than anything, the exact right time to reach the destination. By giving Him charge of the ride, you'll see the most amazing things along the way too. Adventures that you've never imagined.

To be continued... Blessings!

Elder Steve

But as it is written:
"Eye has not seen, nor ear heard, Nor have entered into the heart of man the things which God has prepared for those who love Him."
1 Cor. 2:9

"Call to Me, and I will answer you,
and show you great and mighty things, which you do not know."
Jer. 33:3

"For My thoughts are not your thoughts, nor are your ways My ways,"
says the LORD. "For as the heavens are higher than the earth,
so are My ways higher than your ways,
and My thoughts than your thoughts.
Isaiah 55:8-9

Assurance
Of Salvation Verses
For when doubt arises about God's salvation,
remember who you belong to,
and His promises to those who believe in His Son's name... Jesus.

"But as many as received Him, to them He gave the right to become children of God, to those who believe in His name:" John 1:12

"For God so loved the world that He gave His only begotten Son, that whoever believes in Him should not perish but have everlasting life." John 3:16

"Most assuredly, I say to you, he who hears My word and believes in Him who sent Me has everlasting life, and shall not come into judgment, but has passed from death into life." John 5:24

"And truly Jesus did many other signs in the presence of His disciples, which are not written in this book; but these are written that you may believe that Jesus is the Christ, the Son of God, and that believing you may have life in His name." John 20:30-31

"that if you confess with your mouth the Lord Jesus and believe in your heart that God has raised Him from the dead, you will be saved. For with the heart one believes unto righteousness, and with the mouth confession is made unto salvation. For the Scripture says, "Whoever believes on Him will not be put to shame." For there is no distinction between Jew and Greek, for the same Lord over all is rich to all who call upon Him. For "whoever calls on the name of the LORD shall be saved." Romans 10:9-13

"Let your conduct be without covetousness; be content with such things as you have. For He Himself has said, "I will never leave you nor forsake you." Hebrews 13:5

"And this is the testimony: that God has given us eternal life, and this life is in His Son. He who has the Son has life; he who does not have the Son of God does not have life. These things I have written to you who believe in the name of the Son of God, that you may know that you have eternal life, and that you may continue to believe in the name of the Son of God." 1 John 5:11-13

www.ingramcontent.com/pod-product-compliance
Lightning Source LLC
LaVergne TN
LVHW011223080426
835509LV00005B/293